MY
DOG
IS MY
HERO

EDITED BY
SUSAN REYNOLDS

My

DOG

Is My

HERO

Tributes to the Companions Who Give Us
Love, Loyalty, and a New Leash on Life

Aadamsmedia

AVON, MASSACHUSETTS

Published by
Adams Media, a division of F+W Media, Inc.
57 Littlefield Street, Avon, MA 02322. U.S.A.
www.adamsmedia.com

ISBN 10: 1-60550-362-2
ISBN 13: 978-1-60550-362-2
eISBN 10: 1-4405-0868-2
eISBN 13: 978-1-4405-0868-4

Printed in the United States of America.

10   9   8   7   6   5   4   3   2   1

Library of Congress Cataloging-in-Publication Data
My dog is my hero / edited by Susan Reynolds.
p. cm.
ISBN-13: 978-1-60550-362-2
ISBN-10: 1-60550-362-2
1. Dogs—Anecdotes. 2. Dog owners—Anecdotes. 3. Human-animal relationships—
Anecdotes. I. Reynolds, Susan (Linda Susan)
SF426.2.M93 2010
636.70092'9—dc22
2010019564

This publication is designed to provide accurate and authoritative information with regard
to the subject matter covered. It is sold with the understanding that the publisher is not
engaged in rendering legal, accounting, or other professional advice. If legal advice or
other expert assistance is required, the services of a competent professional person should
be sought.

—From a *Declaration of Principles* jointly adopted by a Committee of the
American Bar Association and a Committee of Publishers and Associations

Many of the designations used by manufacturers and sellers to distinguish their product
are claimed as trademarks. Where those designations appear in this book and Adams
Media was aware of a trademark claim, the designations have been printed with initial
capital letters.

paw print © istockphoto/wellesenterprises

This book is available at quantity discounts for bulk purchases.
For information, please call 1-800-289-0963.

I lovingly dedicate this anthology to Rozanne Reynolds and Brenda Compton, two women with huge hearts and soft spots for dogs. Not only do they take in abandoned and abused dogs, they take excellent care of them and shower them with love. If truth be known, Rozanne is quite the unheralded dog whisperer—there's not a dog alive she can't charm.

And to a little cocker spaniel named Buffy, who left this world years ago but will always be remembered as the sweetest and perfect dog for Brooke and Brett from the day he joined our family on December 25, 1987.

Contents

Acknowledgments / xiii
Introduction / xv

The Ballad of Casey
WILLIAM SCHMITT / 1

Rye to the Rescue
JUDIE FREELAND / 5

Gypsy Gets Her Man
LIBBY SIMON / 9

Not in the Beagle's Neighborhood
PAULA MUNIER / 13

For the Love of Sky and Obie and Skip and
Princess (and Sammie)
ROZANNE REYNOLDS / 19

Traveling Tales
BETH LYNN CLEGG / 25

The Ever-Affable George
DENNIS C. BENTLEY / 29

The Dog Who Eschewed Tennis Balls
BRIAN STAFF / 35

Gibraltar Awash in a Sea of Class Clowns
ROXANNE HAWN / 39

The Country Squire
LUCILLE BELLUCCI / 43

Tribute to Katy
JUDITH GILLE / 49

The Guardian
MITZI L. BOLES / 53

On Tour with the Ambassador
GARY PRESLEY / 57

Turbo, Our Extraordinary Canine Hero
ED KOSTRO / 63

The Amazing Boodini
JAMES E. SCHMID, JR. / 67

Me & My Shadow
ANDREW MCALEER / 71

Gene and Roddy
ALLEN MCGILL / 77

Mozart Must Have Had a Poodle
CASSIE RODGERS / 83

A Dog Named Bum
LARRY CONNER / 87

Queen of My Heart
RUTH ANDREW / 91

Our Unexpected Hero, Schnauzer
JOYCE ROBINSON / 95

Five New Sets of Eyes
JANE ANGELICH / 99

The Widget Dance
KAREN BAKER / 103

When Nat Rescued Nami
TERRI ELDERS / 107

The Labrador Way
LESE DUNTON / 113

The Bond
KATHRYN GODSIFF / 117

Red Dog
LOGAN BRANJORD / 123

Dual Heroines
DAVID L. AUGUSTYN / 127

Honor
NANCY BAKER / 133

Goofy Willy
LINDA O'CONNELL / 137

That Lion-Hearted Brother of Mine
AMRITA DATTA / 143

Our First Child
BILLY CUCHENS / 147

A Matter of Heart
CAROL PATTON / 151

Loyalty on Three Legs
ALLAN REGIER / 155

Kid Land Security
PRISCILLA CARR / 159

Jack and the Mud Pies
JOYCE L. RAPIER / 165

Cleo Saves the Day
PEG RYAN / 171

Brownie: Mrs. Campbell's Electrified Dog
BILL CHEW / 175

A Knight in Furry Armor
ROBERT PAUL BLUMENSTEIN / 181

The Bluebirds of Fife
JOYCE STARK / 187

The Chase
JESSICA BARMACK / 191

Huckleberry, the Unlikely Hero
ALLISON PATTILLO / 197

More Intimidating Than a Plastic Sled
PETE REDINGTON / 201

Love, Seven-Fold
LAD MOORE / 207

Life, A.D. (After Dog)
JAY MAX KRAIDMAN / 213

Dogs Know Things
THOMAS SMITH / 217

Sunday Mornings with Duke
STEPHEN BLACKBURN / 221

In the Company of Elliott
TRACY GRIMALDI / 225

Bumbo the Wonder Dog
KATHRYN THOMPSON PRESLEY / 231

A Letter to My Running Partner
CATHARINE MOSER / 235

Acknowledgments

I would like to thank my children, Brooke and Brett Aved, for always inspiring me to do my best at whatever I attempt. At Adams Media, I'd like to thank Karen Cooper, Paula Munier, Phil Sexton, Beth Gissinger-Rivera, Brendan O'Neill, Matt Glazer, Victoria Sandbrook, and everyone else from production to sales for their enthusiasm and support. I would also like to thank the fifty contributors who shared their stories for all of us to enjoy! Thank you for putting forth your best efforts to bring your beloved dogs to life on the page. Anyone who reads this book will be richer for having done so.

Introduction

Welcome to *My Dog Is My Hero*, a cornucopia of stories about the most unforgettable dogs you'll ever want to meet. While all the stories honor those beloved pets that bring so much to our lives, you'll find marvelous diversity—lots of heroic deeds, humor, and sweetness, with a touch of nostalgia and sadness.

You'll laugh along with Paula Munier when she recounts the story of how her dog protected her against an intrusive neighbor; with Dennis C. Bentley, whose ever-affable George plays a game of catch unlike any other dog and brings endless fun to his loving family as well as to the foster dogs that George unwittingly mentors; and with Roxanne Hawn, as her reluctant border collie, Lilly, makes a big splash in behavior training.

You'll fall in love with Rye, a gentle golden retriever who repeatedly rescues a baby bird by capturing it in his mouth and transporting it to safety; Jeeves, a huge, lumbering mixed breed of Anatolian shepherd and Great Pyrenees who protects a wounded fawn; and Turbo, a crusty old rez (reservation) dog that nurses a sick cat and guards a wounded sparrow.

You'll celebrate the rescue of Obie and Skip and Princess, three lucky dogs who find a loving home—with Sky, a spunky blue rat terrier, and her owners, Rozanne and Brenda—after being badly abused. You'll marvel at the escapades of The Amazing Boodini, a Yorkshire terrier who defies his master's every attempt to contain him. You'll cheer the heroism of Kodiak, a malamute who unwittingly rescues his master lost in a blinding, driving snowstorm.

You'll read about Sheena, a ranch dog in New Zealand who forms a special bond with her owners; the antics of Goofy Willy, a half hound dog and half husky in Alaska; Sheri, a dog in India who steals a young girl's heart and helps her survive her parents' separation; Roy, a cross between a collie and an Alsation in Scotland who still lives in his owner's heart fifty years after his passing; and Totó, a roving mutt in Brazil that weasels his way into Lucille Bellucci's heart.

And, of course, we have a-boy-and-his-dog stories, including Logan Branjord's Red Dog, who skidded on and fell through ice to save another dog, and Stephen Blackburn's nostalgic *Sunday Mornings with Duke* that rings true to many.

We also have dogs such as Shadow, a rescued three-legged mutt who helps Andrew McAleer's dying parents feel comforted in their waning days, and then helps Andrew as he struggles through debilitating cancer treatments; and Mozart, an American Eskimo puppy who tricks his master, who has debilitating heart problems, into exercising.

We even have a famous dog—Honor, the golden retriever who dialed the hospital when her wheelchair-bound master was injured by a falling beam.

Although it's always sad when a beloved dog leaves the world—our world—it's something all pet owners face someday. Without dwelling on the pathos, we included a few farewell stories, including Judith Gille's *Tribute to Katy*, which offers a lovely, eloquent tribute to her unforgettable golden retriever, and Jessica Barmack's *The Chase*, which says an elegant farewell to her beloved and resilient Sam.

All this and so much more awaits you. Enjoy!

The Ballad of Casey

WILLIAM SCHMITT

I used to tell people that my first child had four legs and pointy ears. This distinguished him from my later children, who had two legs and pointy ears. Like many childless couples, my wife and I treated our dog, Casey, more like a person than a pet. He was a spirited little guy whose personality won me over when I had intended to purchase another puppy. Not long after we brought him home, however, we discovered that "spirited" was another word for "having a mind of my own."

Casey had a real thing about being left behind. The first time we had the audacity to do this, he literally chewed a windowsill off. Because we were renting an apartment at the time, this posed a problem. The next time, we thought we might as well take the little rascal with us; unfortunately, we again had the audacity to leave him in our car while we visited with friends for a few hours. He ate the driver's seat. He didn't chew it up—he ate it. There was nothing but springs and a few leather shreds left when we returned. Somehow, we still loved him, which said a lot for his personality *most* of the time. Casey was a little, cocky mutt with a Type A personality, and this eventually brought him into direct conflict with our neighbor dog.

The first time I laid eyes on this neighbor dog, I had just stepped outside on an early October morning. We had rented a really old farmhouse, with windowsills that looked like they came prechewed. There, in the foggy mist of a crisp, clear autumn morn, standing about fifteen feet away, was this huge wolflike creature, staring at me with one eye. I say one eye, because his other eye was all white, most likely blinded in a vicious street fight. If a dog as big and mean-looking as this dog was on the losing end, he must have tangled with a grizzly bear.

I quickly stepped forward, took a commanding, authoritative stance and sternly pronounced, "Get out of here." Neighbor dog showed no signs of being intimidated. In fact, he never moved a muscle; he simply glared at me, as though he was trying to figure out whether he could eat me in two bites or three. In another stern, authoritative voice I blurted, "Welcome to our yard." Apparently, he was so well-trained he was not disposed to spoil his own yard with his necessary duties. Our yard must have seemed like a giant outhouse to him, as that appeared to be the main reason for his regular visits.

Our little Casey would never be in the neighbor dog's size category. In fact, Casey wasn't very big at all. But when he looked into a mirror, he didn't see a little, white, pointy-eared mutt—he saw a bull mastiff, the terror of the neighborhood. So Casey had no trepidation about visiting this neighbor dog's yard. When I let him out, he went sniffing about the bushes on the border of old one-eye's yard. I could see old one-eye lying under a tree observing Casey. He didn't bark (the grizzly could have ripped his tongue out for all I knew), but I could see him as he tensed his body, preparing to strike. I realized what was coming, even if my little Captain Oblivious couldn't, so I called for Casey to come back. This occurred many years before I knew anything about dog whispering, so an undisciplined, insensitive Casey felt no obligation to heed my call. The one-eyed werewolf continued to quietly fix his steely gaze on my dumb dog, but he didn't move until Casey uncorked his John Hancock on the bush.

Jack Nicholson's Joker character in *Batman* warns Bruce Wayne to "Never rub another man's rhubarb," and Casey had just done this. The one-eyed hound from hell took off after our little mutt, no doubt figuring this would be a one-bite lunch. Now Casey was nothing if not fast, and he whipped across the road, darting and dodging in every direction, dashing madly toward the relative safety of our yard. Almost made it, too. But just as he cleared the road to our yard, the big bad wolf gave him a good sharp chomp on his butt. I worried that Casey's time had come, but the big dog decided to let the little whelp off with a warning: *Just because I mess in your yard doesn't mean you can mess in mine.* I began to suspect that he worked for our government.

My wife and I treated this situation like we would treat similar situations when we had real children: We looked over the boo-boo to make sure he wasn't really hurt, fussed over him for a few minutes until he felt a little better, and then we laughed and made fun of him. I was so impressed by the little guy's gumption that I wrote a little song called *The Ballad of Casey*, which I sung, with apologies, to the tune of Johnny Cash's *Folsom Prison Blues*.

I see my dog a'comin'
He's comin' round the bend
The one-eyed dog is after him
Biting his rear end.

WILLIAM SCHMITT lives with his wife in Upstate New York. He teaches English by phone to European businesspeople, and writes part time under the name The Hermit Crab. He has four sons and one grandson.

Rye to the Rescue

JUDIE FREELAND

Rye loved sparrows, robins, barn swallows, pheasants, ducks, and every other kind of bird. She was a retriever, after all, a golden retriever with a very soft mouth. That meant that she could pick up a bird—a sparrow, a robin, a barn swallow, a pheasant, or a duck—so gently that it would be held but never hurt.

One spring, a young robin appeared in our yard. His mother was trying to teach him to fly. She sat with her baby near a corner at the top of the chain-link fence around our dog yard. Then she flew just past the corner to perch again on the top of the fence. She coaxed the young robin to fly to her. He tried, but not hard enough. He fluttered to the ground.

Rye had just gone out into the dog yard with me. She saw the bird sitting on the ground and did what any good bird dog would do: Very gently, she picked up the young robin and wiggled her tongue so he could sit on it, gently caged between her teeth, then brought him to me.

Rye sat in front of me, looking like she had a hot potato in her mouth. I held out my hand and asked her to "Release." She tried, but it was impossible to just spit the baby robin out. She looked up with a "Help me, Mom" look in her eye. So I cautiously opened her mouth wide and saw the baby robin sitting on Rye's tongue. I also saw the mother robin in great distress, fluttering from one fence post to another and cheeping frantically.

I lifted the baby robin from Rye's mouth, carried it out the gate, and set it on the ground away from the fence. Mother robin swooped down, chirping loudly, as if scolding her baby (as mothers will do when convinced that their babies are in danger) and scuttled it away into the tall grass.

There were more flying lessons. And Rye retrieved the young robin four more times. I had named him Robbie, since by this time he was almost part of the family. Four more times I put Robbie outside the fence. And mother robin fussed. I thought she was afraid the chick would never learn to fly and some other creature would eat her baby. Perhaps she trusted that Rye would rescue Robbie and would not hurt him. But still she had to scold. Maybe she told him that not all creatures would cradle him between sharp teeth on a warm, wet tongue. That some creatures would eat him, as he ate worms.

Finally, Robbie got the necessary skills to fly from one part of the fence to another, then he learned to fly longer and longer distances.

Some weeks later, Robbie had an accident. He was now big and a good flier. He looked almost like his mother, but his breast was still baby-speckled. He had learned to find worms and to find water in puddles on the ground after rain. He also had learned where to find water when there was no rain—in a big tub in our horse pasture that was always full of water. He could perch on the edge of the tub and lean over just a little bit to get a drink. Rye and I had seen him several evenings when we went to the pasture to check the fences and get some exercise.

One evening, when there had been no rain, so there were no rain puddles, Robbie flew to the big tub. The water was not as close to the top as he may have hoped. The horses had been drinking it, and it had not yet been refilled.

Later, I could imagine how it happened. He leaned over. He leaned over farther. Not quite close enough. He leaned over more. He fell in! He could not get out! The top of the tub was too far to reach. His feathers were getting waterlogged. His head was in danger of going under. He was going to drown! He probably cheeped in panic. But his mother was not near enough to hear him, and she could not have helped if she had heard. Robbie was probably trying to flap his wings, kicking his feet in terror, and struggling to hold his head up.

Rye and I had just come through the pasture gate. I didn't hear anything, but her keen ears did. I watched her run to the water trough and stick her head over the rim to pick something out of the water and set it on the ground. Then she looked at me and barked, shrilly, insistently.

I ran over to where Robbie crouched, bedraggled and dripping. I pulled tufts of grass and tried to pat him dry before making a warm little nest of grass. I laid the tiny body inside and set it outside the fence, knowing that Rye would retrieve her little friend again if she could, and right then was not a good time.

Rye and I watched as Robbie sat in his makeshift nest and shivered. Slowly, his feathers dried and he began to flutter his wings. Finally, he launched himself. He could fly again! Just as he rose into the air, he turned and chirped as if to say, "Thank you."

Although Robbie had evidently learned his lesson and didn't return to the trough, Rye checked it every evening for the next few days, ready to rescue her feathered friend yet again should it be necessary.

JUDIE FREELAND has authored two scholarly books and numerous articles, a critical bibliography of Tolkien criticism, and a memoir about her father. She is a retired English professor living with her therapy dog, Echo. The heroine of this story has gone to the Rainbow Bridge.

Gypsy Gets Her Man

LIBBY SIMON

Little did I know when I started out on an ordinary family vacation it would end with guns and police, and at the center of it all would be a little miniature black poodle called Gypsy. It all began with an invitation from my brother Sam and sister-in-law Katie to come for a visit. I jumped at the opportunity and soon found myself on a flight to Fort Lauderdale, Florida.

When I arrived at their front door, I was "attacked" by this unexpected new addition to their family. Midnight black with two piercing brown eyes, this little dynamo zinged like a lightning bolt right to my heart. A mischievous, playful bundle of fur, Gypsy had boundless energy that never seemed to wane. We took to each other right away, and she quickly taught me to play her favorite game: "catch the Frisbee." Every day she led the way to the local park to play. In the apartment, she entertained herself by clenching the Frisbee between her teeth, vigorously shaking it with her head and flinging it into the air. Off she scampered following its flight, over and under the furniture, wherever it took her. The days flew by quickly, and Gypsy had me pretty well trained by the time I was to return home.

On my last day, Gypsy lured me to the park one more time to play Frisbee. We returned home to rest before a planned evening I was to spend with my hosts. Gypsy devoured her dinner before we left and, almost purring like a cat, curled up in her favorite easy chair with her precious toy. She had the run of the house when her "parents" went out, and we had every reason to presume she would be a very responsible, reliable watchdog.

After a pleasant evening, we arrived home quite late. As the three of us started up the stairs, we could hear Gypsy snarling and growling ferociously. This was strange! She rarely barked, especially with such vigor, unless something or someone triggered her. Something was very wrong! Sam cautiously opened the front door a crack. Three pairs of eyes peered inside to see Gypsy on her haunches, nose pointing at the center of a bifold closet in the entryway, yipping incessantly, her paws scratching on the doors in a wild frenzy. She was so engrossed she remained totally unaware of our presence. We looked at one another with one thought but not a word: A thief had obviously come into the house and had been caught in the act. He must have hidden in the closet and was now trapped by Gypsy. Sam closed the door quietly, and we sneaked back down the stairs. While Sam ran to the neighbors to phone the police, Katie and I hid under the staircase to watch in case the robber managed to escape his yappy but determined captor.

Within minutes, the police arrived. Two big, burly police officers approached silently.

"No one has come out yet," I whispered. "He must still be in there."

"It's a two-story drop from a second-floor window because this is a duplex," added my sister-in-law in a hushed tone. "There is no other way out."

The two officers, with the three of us in tow, stealthily climbed the stairs and opened the door just enough to reveal Gypsy still wildly barking and scraping the bifold wooden doors. The police stepped inside and positioned themselves on each side of the closet. With guns drawn and pointed at the tiny prison cell, they signaled to each other with a head nod and flung open both doors—simultaneously Gypsy pounced! Instantly her teeth sunk into . . . the . . . Frisbee!? We all watched in disbelief as Gypsy bounded across the room, Frisbee clenched tightly between her teeth, and jumped into her easy chair with the quiet satisfaction of a mission accomplished. We were stunned, speechless, and red-faced—but not as crimson as the police.

How did that Frisbee get into the closet? We later surmised that she must have been playing her usual game of catch by herself. She likely flung it up and on landing, it slid under the doors. She was unable to retrieve it, and hence the scene we had witnessed upon our return.

I would have loved to read the incidence report the police filed that night. They really didn't need to worry about us revealing the embarrassing incident, because to expose them would also have implicated us.

It was best to let sleeping dogs lie.

LIBBY SIMON is a retired social worker living in Winnipeg, Canada, who has become a freelance writer. Her works include humor and slice-of-life stories that have been published in newspapers, magazines and anthologies in Canada and the United States.

Not in the Beagle's Neighborhood

PAULA MUNIER

I n most every neighborhood, there's one neglected house that all the other homeowners on the street complain is bringing down their property values. On the isolated road that runs along the lake where we live, that house was a tiny cottage with peeling paint, junk cluttering the driveway, and thigh-high weeds for a yard. Worse, the tenants were often seen being escorted from the property by local law enforcement, only to return a few days later. But to our collective relief, eventually they disappeared for good, and a "for sale" sign went up on the lot. Not that we could imagine anyone actually buying the house in its unkempt condition.

The little cottage stood empty for months. Then one happy day, a truck pulled up, a guy got out, and the renovation began. He gutted the place and transformed it from derelict cabin to lakeside jewel in a matter of weeks. We were thrilled and predisposed to like the bachelor who'd cleaned up the worst house on the block.

He was a friendly, attractive guy, happy to discuss the details of the cottage's rebirth. I met him as I walked my dogs, Shakespeare and Freddie, down the road to the bogs for our daily excursion into the great outdoors. Shakespeare, a big, cheerful mutt from the pound who liked everyone, wagged his tail. Freddie, a small beagle suspicious of any man outside our immediate family, growled and barked, lunging on the leash. I held the aggressive little dog back while I shouted a welcome to our new neighbor over Freddie's loud howls, then moved quickly on my way.

That evening the new neighbor knocked on our door, prompting the usual cacophony of growls and barks and howls from Freddie. I'd done everything to train Freddie to respond better to strangers at the door. Once he'd actually snapped at a longtime family friend—a gentle man who loved dogs and whom Freddie should have recognized—as the poor guy entered our home. We went to obedience classes—where we were asked to leave. We tried special collars—which Freddie chewed to bits. We consulted the vet—who prescribed puppy Prozac. Nothing worked. Freddie was a sweet and loving dog to women everywhere and the few men whom he deemed family—and an aggressive and unpredictable hound from hell to most every other man on the planet, neighbors included. I was thinking about building a fence around my property; with Freddie around, maybe good fences did make good neighbors. Not to mention then I could add a doggie door, giving Freddie twenty-four-hour access to the outdoors, which might cut back on his "accidents." But I hated to ruin the view.

I held Freddie back as I answered the door.

"Hi," said the neighbor we'll call M.

"Hi," I said, holding on to Freddie for dear life. "Sorry."

"No problem, I like dogs."

"Yeah, well, he doesn't like men much."

M looked at me and grinned. "That's not good."

"No." I laughed. "It's not."

"I'd love to come in and see your place."

"Oh, of course." I backed away from the door with Freddie. "Sure, come on in." I pulled Freddie into the living room, and with Shakespeare on my heels, pointed to their doggie pillows in the corner.

"Bed," I said. Since sleeping is Freddie's favorite pastime—after eating, that is—he curled right up next to Shakespeare, keeping one eye on M as he did.

I turned to M. "Would you like a beer or something?"

"Sure. Thanks." M sat down on my couch in front of the fireplace as if he owned the place. "This is a great house."

"Thanks. You've certainly done a lot with yours." I handed him a beer and sat down at the other end of the L-shaped sectional.

With that opening, M was off and running. He told me how he'd inherited some money, checked out the local foreclosures, and found the house on our street. What a mess the place was, the complete remodeling he had to do, how much hard work it took to make it a habitable home. "But it was all worth it," he said. "I always wanted to live on this lake."

"Yes, it's lovely here."

"So," he said, suddenly switching gears and leaning toward me. "You're single, aren't you?"

"Uh, yes."

"Wow, what luck." He leered at me. "I move into my new place, and right away I meet a babe." And with that lame preamble he fell on me, all tongue and hands and heavy breathing.

I pushed him off me and stood up. "You need to leave now."

He held his hands up. "Hey, just being neighborly, you know?"

"You need to leave now," I repeated.

He started toward me, his arms open now in a welcoming embrace. "I mean, you're single, I'm single—"

"Now," I said, with a firmness that brought Freddie to his feet. The fierce little beagle rocketed across the room, fangs bared.

"Whoa," called M, backing up.

I caught Freddie by the collar as he zipped past me, just as he lunged at M's crotch. I jerked him back just as his jaws began to close around M's hands, which the terrified man had cupped around his private parts. "You can let yourself out."

"Maybe another time," M said, regaining his composure as he slipped out my front door, Freddie howling and growling all the while, Shakespeare's deep baritone bark now adding to the din.

"I don't think so," I said as I locked the door behind him.

"That's enough," I told the dogs, and Shakespeare stopped barking. Freddie, naturally, did not.

"Enough," I said again. Freddie quieted down, gazed up at me with those big, innocent brown eyes and then looked down, penitent, ready for his punishment. This is the part where I usually chastised him with more than one "Bad dog! Bad dog! Bad dog!"

But tonight I surprised us both by going to the fridge and pulling out two slices of American cheese, Shakespeare's and Freddie's favorite "people food" treat.

While the dogs chomped down dessert, I poured myself a glass of wine and raised it in a mock toast to the world's worst beagle:

"To Freddie, who knows a good neighbor when he sees one—or not."

Freddie wagged his tail in acknowledgment of my praise—and promptly lifted his leg against the kitchen cabinet.

Time to build that fence.

PAULA MUNIER has been a dog person her whole life. Raised by a man with a penchant for Weimaraners, vizslas, and Great Danes, on her tenth birthday she got her first dog of her own—a black miniature poodle named Rogue. Since then she has shared her life with numerous dogs, cats, fish, and a bearded lizard, all of which together caused far less trouble than just one small beagle named Freddie. This story was excerpted from her memoir, *Fixing Freddie*, published by Adams Media in Fall 2010.

For the Love of Sky and Obie and Skip and Princess (and Sammie)

ROZANNE REYNOLDS

Ever since my daughter's cat, Sammie, became sick (three years prior) and came to live with us (temporarily, we thought), we had no desire for a dog. But when Brenda and I spotted the most adorable litter of pure-blood blue rat terriers for sale at a flea market, we simply fell in love with the runt of the litter. A smart, cute puppy, she soon became the apple of our eyes—and the queen of our household. We called our new baby Sky, although her registered name was Sophia Sky Blue Compton-Reynolds, and we all lived very happily together until fate brought us exactly what we thought we didn't want— a household of dogs.

Several families in the nearby countryside hired Brenda, a commercial Realtor, to sell their property. On a site visit, Brenda discovered one of these families had a small pack of dogs that were malnourished and covered with fleas. They claimed to love their dogs, but they weren't in a financial position to care for them. Brenda and I volunteered to take the dogs—one or two at a time—to have them spayed or neutered and to get all their shots.

A few weeks later, as Brenda and I arrived with flea and tick medicine, one of the men told Brenda that he had struck the family's brown dog with his car. When he said he was waiting for the dog to "crawl off into the woods to die," and then laughed, Brenda and I looked at each other and wordlessly agreed that we would take the dog—and never return him. A boy around ten or eleven offered to find him and soon returned carrying an emaciated, bedraggled, fly-bitten, pitiful-looking dog that immediately stole my heart. After we lay him in the back of our SUV, I crawled in beside him to comfort him as we sped to the emergency animal clinic.

After an examination, the veterinarian told us he was a full-grown half pit bull/half Labrador who had withered away to seventeen pounds, that his leg was broken in two places and that he would require a long recovery. Brenda and I had agreed that naming him would likely mean that we would never give him up; so when the vet asked his name, I waited to see what Brenda would do. She hemmed and hawed, and then said, "Obie . . . because I once knew a dog named Obie and I always liked the name." To me, our rescue embodied Obi-Wan Kenobi, the wise one from the *Star Wars* series. Clearly, he had stolen both of our hearts.

Nevertheless, after his surgery, we told ourselves that we would adopt him out as soon as he was well. To prevent Sky and Sammie from bothering him, we settled him into the basement, attached a long lead to a supporter, gave him a big bowl of food and lots of water, and left the basement door open. Unfortunately, Sky begged to go out onto the deck, where she nudged her nose so tightly between the boards, straining to see Obie, we thought she'd never get it out. After a few days, we all surrendered and brought Obie into the house. We drove our new dog to the vet every week for months to have his cast replaced. He was there so often, as soon as I dropped his leash, he walked back to "his room" and stepped inside the cage. He loved going because they all fawned over him, but we all did. Underneath the dirt and fly bites and skeletal frame beat the very loving heart of a very precious dog.

Three years later, Obie is a beautiful reddish-brown color and is the most loving, sociable, protective dog you would ever want to meet. When Obie sees us, he comes toward us just a-licking. He will shower his love on us—or anyone he likes—bathing our hands, arms, and legs until we beg him to stop. Obie loves me so much; I swear he has wrinkled the skin on my legs and arms. Obie has Addison's disease, and he cannot handle good or bad stress without monthly shots and daily steroid pills. He is our 60-pound special needs baby.

Another time—at the same clients' property—we noticed that an all-white pit bull/boxer puppy, with a big black patch over his left eye, was encrusted with so much dirt he looked black. When we asked why his belly was swollen, they admitted that they had poured lye down his throat in a thwarted attempt to rid him of worms. We scooped him up and took him to the vet, where he was properly treated for worms and given the care he so desperately needed. Even though they wanted him back, we staunchly refused. We named him "Skip" because we love the movie *My*

Dog Skip and because, when he gets excited (which he does all the time), he actually skips. He reminds everyone of Petey from the Little Rascals gang or Nipper, the RCA Victor dog.

Our Skip is sweet, shy, and timid. If anyone raises his or her voice or a loud noise startles him, Skip runs as far away from the noise as possible and cowers. Recently, the city was paving our streets, and on our daily walk a loud construction noise startled Skip. Six or seven workers were standing on a low wall when Skip hopped over it and scurried down the other side at such a rapid pace, his leash swept the entire row of men off the wall. Fortunately, they just laughed.

Like Obie, once Skip recovered, he became a playful little guy. He loves to come up behind you, put his front legs around your neck, and then lick your neck and nibble your ears. He developed a habit of jutting his lower jaw out and showing his bottom teeth, or flashing what we call his "Elvis sneer" by having his canine tooth on one side or the other of his mouth showing. For the most part, he is very docile, but he does love to play, much to Obie's and Sky's dismay at times. His idea of playing is to run up behind the other dogs and nip their hind legs. When they turn around to object, he tucks his stub of a tail flat against his little behind and scoots away. When I travel, I often take Skip and Obie with me because they travel so well, they enjoy each other's company, and they get along extremely well with other dogs and people. Skip has never met a dog he didn't like. Skip is our 45-pound lover boy.

We have since rescued several other dogs and adopted them out, but when Princess, Skip's pit bull mother, needed us, of course we took her in—she's our sweet survivor girl. When I walk all four of our dogs—twice a day—people assume I am a professional dog walker. When I recount each dog's story, they tell me there will be a place in heaven for Brenda and me, but I tell them that we did it for the dogs, not any rewards, and that their different personalities and quirks have become our treasures. They have shown us how much anyone shines once love and care clear away abuse and neglect, and that all anyone needs is someone to love him or her properly. Each of our dogs is precious to us, and us to them. They deserved a loving home and a good life, and now they have it. But we're not the heroes—they are.

ROZANNE REYNOLDS lives in Raleigh, North Carolina, with four dogs, a cat, and Brenda. Since her children also love dogs, a family reunion often has more dogs than humans in attendance. Rozanne's first story appeared in *Woodstock Revisited: 50 Far Out, Groovy, Peace-Loving, Flashback-Inducing Stories from Those Who Were There.* She encourages everyone to adopt abused dogs and promises that these special dogs will bring you far more love than you can ever give to them.

Traveling Tales

BETH LYNN CLEGG

A mixed-breed, shorthaired puppy greeted me when I arrived at my paternal grandmother's home to celebrate my seventh birthday. Separated as we were by one house, the worn path through my neighbor's backyard was evidence of my frequent post-birthday visits to Grandma's and the agreement we had reached: The puppy would live with her, but we'd share his training so I could learn how to take care of a dog. I was overjoyed and agreed that we had to choose a name befitting this handsome pup with a white coat accentuated by black ears and muzzle. We called out several to see how they'd sound when we wanted him to come to us. I have no recollection of what prompted me to choose the one that stuck, but looking back, it's logical. Grandmother was my hero, and she had given him to me. We named him Hero.

Grandmother Miller had heredity deafness and lived alone, so if she wasn't wearing her hearing aide she often missed phone calls or a knock on the door. That changed when Hero became part of the household. During the day, he stayed inside, where his outside bark was allowed, even encouraged. If Grandmother didn't respond, he grabbed the hem of her garment and ran to the door or the phone, yipping as if to say, "Look what I can do!" Grandmother said she slept better at night knowing Hero lay on the porch beneath her bedroom window. When we told Hero he was smart and a good dog, he would jump up and down before running around in circles with a look on his face that could only be described as a smile.

By his first year, Hero weighed about twenty pounds. His medium-sized, sleek muscular body and long legs didn't match the German police breed that had to be part of the mix, even though he certainly displayed the breed's loyalty and fearlessness. Grandmother and I spent many hours in her beautiful front garden under his watchful eye. When someone came down the sidewalk, Hero sprang into action, even if it was all bark and no bite. After we looked up, he stood, with tail wagging, position unchanged, between us and whoever approached. Hero knew everyone in the neighborhood, and many stopped to praise him as our protector, sending his curved tail into eggbeater mode.

As the neighborhood tomboy, when I wasn't climbing trees or playing cowboys and Indians, I was roller-skating or pushing my homemade scooter. Once Grandmother said, "Go along with my little darling," and thus Hero became my guardian, racing beside me until we both collapsed on her front steps, where Grandmother greeted me with a treat, most times a glass of fresh lemonade and warm cookies. Hero would make a dash for his water bowl and then return to sprawl spread-eagle on his belly, tongue hanging out of his mouth, his eyes pleading with me to give it a rest.

A new routine for Hero and me began on my tenth Christmas, when I found a bicycle beside the tree. For a couple of years, we became a familiar sight for blocks around the University of Texas neighborhoods as we traversed them almost daily during the summer, including those first few days of June 1942 as Grandmother's life slipped away.

After mother shared the news I'd been dreading, most of that time was lost in a blur, save for my immediate response, which remains vivid. I grabbed Hero, pressed my face into his neck, and hugged him until he gave a soft yelp and squirmed for release. I hadn't intended to hurt him, and he quickly reassured me by licking tears from my cheeks. With no siblings to lean on and parents who were unable to express or share their feelings, Hero became the receptacle of my grief-stricken words. He sat still, black eyes riveted on mine, head tilted sideways, with one ear cocked as if he understood. He became my best friend, and I shared everything with him as I'd done with Grandmother. Since she'd believed he would protect me, I accepted it as truth.

By the end of summer, we'd explored areas of town far beyond home base. On one of those excursions, in a matter of seconds I discovered what I'd known all along: Hero was appropriately named. As I peddled down a busy street, he made a sudden dash forward, forcing me to make an abrupt right turn on a side street. While fighting to maintain control of my bike, I prepared to scold him when the sound of squealing tires stopped me cold. A car traveling behind us had lost control and ended up on the sidewalk in the area where we would've been. Once again, as words of thanks spilled out in torrents, my hugs left Hero squirming for release. I still have no answer for how or why he sensed danger, only gratitude that he did.

As my focus shifted from tomboy activities to activities involving boys, Hero and I shared fewer traveling times, but he was always waiting when I arrived home, ready for words of praise and a treat. In ten eventful years, I never lost a sense of Grandmother's presence whenever I poured out my heart to my best friend. And Hero always stood ready to protect and defend, or to lovingly lick tears from my cheeks.

BETH LYNN CLEGG is a late-blooming, septuagenarian writer who's amazed when her fiction, nonfiction, poetry, and prose is published in a variety of genre such as *A Cup of Comfort® for Friends*, *A Cup of Comfort® Cookbook*, *Charity: True Stories of Giving and Receiving*, and *Nesting, It's a Chick Thing*. She enjoys time with her children, grandchildren, friends, spoiled granddog, and rotten cat.

The Ever-Affable George

DENNIS C. BENTLEY

He yelped, jumping back from the large hole in the dirt he'd poked his head into and dropped to the ground, vigorously rubbing his face on the grass. My wife, Angel, saw this and ran toward him, crawled under the deck, and peered into the hole just as a fair-sized copperhead snake slithered back into it. She grabbed the writhing and moaning dog by the collar, dragged him into the house, grabbed her purse and keys, dragged him out to the car, shoved him into the back seat, and sped to the vet. He sat in the back, moaning, pawing at his swelling jowl, his thick, heavy slobber dripping down to the floorboard.

He asked for it. He really did. He loves everything and everybody. He routinely hauls toads around, yet they all hop out of his mouth unharmed. It is exactly this uncommon fearlessness, gentleness, and respect for other creatures that frequently earn him "Employee-of-the-Month" status at my wife's dog boarding/training/rescue/foster enterprise.

A bright-white, thick-furred dog about the size and shape of a Labrador retriever, he'd come to us as a temporary foster from a humane society shelter. We'd named him Georgio, in honor of the regal Hungarian breed (kuvasz) he most physically resembled (in the rescue business, "most resembles" is about as good as you are ever going to get). After just a few days, watching him prance and leap around the yard, chasing butterflies and yapping at birds, clumsily tripping over everything in his path, we decided on the simpler, more befitting George.

He immediately bonded with our permanent dogs, even old Max. Actually, Max merely tolerated George, and George respected Max's curmudgeonly mood swings. Bailey, the matron aunt of the pack, a Great Pyrenees mix with an alarming baritone bark, even played with George, till she tired of his antics as well. She could simply snap at him once, and George would take off immediately for adventures elsewhere. He never showed signs of aggression, not any. In fact, Angel was concerned that he might be a bit too trusting and carefree. That and his complete lack of critical thinking skills made him a cause for light-hearted concern.

"Watch this," my wife called to me from the deck one evening. She tossed his favorite toy, which to George simply meant the thing currently being tossed. He charged off the deck, barely making the turns and short stairs. He ran out to the yard, but nowhere near where the toy fell.

"He saw it land, why is he searching over there?" I asked her.

"You'll see," she replied, snickering.

After sniffing around, circling, arcing ever wider in his desperate search, he finally found it and in three bounds or less, barely touching the ground, brought back the dripping, slobbery toy.

George watched, very impatiently focused, as she tossed it again to another part of the yard. He ran again, down the stairs and around the corner, kicking up the dust, stopping at the exact wrong area of the yard, where he once again appeared stymied and confused.

"What the . . . " was all I could manage.

"He always goes to the last place he found it," she said with a laugh.

"But he *saw* it; he *watched* it land over there before he started running!" I was baffled.

"Whatever breeds he is a product of," she declared, "this particular dog would never make it in the wild. The squirrels and bunnies would have him figured out in no time at all."

As other foster dogs came and went, it became apparent that George was actually quite handy. Many of the dogs rescued are "dumpster dogs." These dogs are found stray, scavenging around available sources of food. In the human world that they live in, this means dumpsters and trash cans in neighborhoods and parks. This reclusive lifestyle leads many strays to become shy and untrusting. Once they're rescued, this behavior pattern can be difficult to overcome. It requires time, patience and socialization. Dumpster dogs are generally unfamiliar with human touch, stairs, tile floors, doors, and a host of other domestic features. Often they need a guide, another dog to watch, a nonthreatening companion to coax them into overcoming frightening and unfamiliar challenges. Meet George, the mentor.

George never mastered scholastic achievement. It has been very tough to train him to do anything. George's talent lies completely within the moment, within the selfless, blissful universe in which he lives—where all objects are toys, all creatures are friends. Around people, he likes to have his head rubbed, and he happily tolerates it for hours, twisting and contorting his head into your hand so as to get all the good spots, tongue dangling out the side of his face, slobber dripping profusely. If you ever rub his head, he will soon thank you by bringing you something to toss. We caution everyone: "Do not do this! Once you start tossing his toy, the game never, ever, ever ends . . . ever!"

As we brought other foster dogs through, our loopy George adopted each and every one as his new best friend. From a six-week-old litter of eight yapping coonhounds, to a neurotic, yet harmless old pit bull, to a seven-month-old, three-legged terrier mix recovering from amputation. All of these lucky timid animals got to spend a lot of time with George. Scores of dogs over the past four years found new homes, thanks in great part to the tireless efforts of an oblivious, joyful, big white dog that no one else wanted.

The day after he rooted his nose in the copperhead's hole, George lay swollen-faced in his crate, drugged and achy. He watched his buddies come and go for a few days till the medicine finally kicked in and the swelling subsided. As soon as he could, he was back at it again . . . leaping and running around the yard, chasing things only he could see. The little black shepherd,

Katie Sue, followed him, nipping at his heels, George responding in kind. When Angel stepped into the yard, the very shy Katie Sue ran around and cowered, behind her protector—the, brave, noble, ever-affable George.

DENNIS C. BENTLEY, by profession an IT consultant, lives in rural Jefferson County, Missouri, with his wife, Angel, who is a certified trainer and board member of the Coalition for Animal Rescue and Education in Hillsboro. They have four permanent dogs and usually two or three fosters. Dennis also had stories published in *My Teacher Is My Hero* and *My Dad Is My Hero.*

The Dog Who Eschewed Tennis Balls

BRIAN STAFF

The dinner party was stretching into the early hours of the morning. The brandy- and coffee-drinking stage was well underway, the conversation becoming more entertaining (to me at least) as the alcohol loosened the inhibitions that usually restrain polite people from discussing differences in politics or religion, or how their way was *the only proper way* to raise children.

From where I was sitting, I had a clear view of Mogs, the hosts' family dog, sprawled nearby, practically swamping the six-foot shag-pile rug beside the crackling fire. Her back thighs lay spread-eagled behind her like a broken string puppet's. Her head was burrowed between her furry paws, as if she were shielding her eyes. The only time she moved her head all evening was when the feminist of the group spouted her theory on dogs, calling them "wiser than men." And then Mogs merely perked an ear. Throughout the rest of the evening, she remained nonplussed. When our hostess brought the filet mignon through from the kitchen, Mogs lifted her head briefly to flex one nostril. When one of the guests offered a box of expensive chocolate truffles to accompany the first pot of coffee, Mogs seemed to frown. But when I placed a plate of the finest, dark Belgian chocolates on the table, Mogs heaved her 53-pound frame onto her four legs, padded toward the table, and coyly sat at an aloof distance, her eyes drowsily but unblinkingly focused on the plate of chocolates. There, I said to myself, is a dog with discrimination.

Mogs was an old English sheepdog. At least that's how the casual observer would describe her. In my view, she was an elderly, world-weary, wryly cynical professor of philosophy reincarnated as a canine, destined to spend this life placidly contemplating the idiotic goings-on in the human world. When young, Mogs had been mad as a hatter and twice as full of mischief as any other fun-filled pup; but she soon put youthful indiscretions disdainfully to one side and settled into her true vocation—observation and resignation.

On my many visits at the end of each day, I would watch Mogs saunter into the living room, look around, plunk her heavy body down on the rug . . . and sigh. Yes, sigh. To me, her sigh spoke volumes, as if she had witnessed another day amid the existential chaos that we call "life," and her only comment, the perfect comment, was that profound sigh. On such occasions, it required tremendous restraint to stop myself from falling on the floor, hugging Mogs, and exclaiming, "Yes, Mogs. You're absolutely right! What on earth *is* the point?" But I could no more prostrate myself at her paws than I could rush up to a female professor at college and embrace her as she explained Camus or Sartre or Genet to me.

Once, Mogs's cohabitants (she clearly did not consider them owners) decided to have her groomed. Not so much to tidy her up, but more out of a desire to see what she looked like under a matted coat that had collected an array of foliage, mud, cat food remnants, and an assortment of droppings common to areas where chickens, cows, and goats roam. I was there when Mogs came home after the ordeal, and she looked truly beautiful but quintessentially miserable, like a spoiled rich girl who has discovered that money can buy glamour easily enough, but happiness? Never.

Mogs's attitude toward games was disparaging, to say the least. I often witnessed ingenuous strangers pick up a balding tennis ball and throw it for Mogs to retrieve. While the hosts' cat loved the tennis ball, even oddly treated it as if it were her kitten, Mogs's reaction was to invariably ignore the trajectory of the ball, choosing instead to sink to the ground, as if rooting into the earth so the delusional ball tosser would get the message that a sensible dog simply does not chase soiled, hairy tennis balls. Mogs's expression on such occasions (to those who were privileged—or imaginative enough—to understand her) said, *You want me to chase a tennis ball? Would you chase a tennis ball and bring it back to me? Do you have nothing better to do? Please, act your age.*

Mogs was a large dog and I often saw her swallowing every morsel of her food in gulps, but if the cat or a greedy visiting canine interrupted her dining, she would turn aside from her food, dismissing anything the offending animal found appealing as an irrelevance, as if she were above the riffraff who would squabble over a dish of food. To Mogs, such action was akin to someone throwing a drowning man a bagel instead of a life jacket. She had no use for such simple-minded shenanigans.

In reality, Mogs led an uncomplicated life. She slept in the hallway, always in the same place, where I, and many others, would clumsily step over her bulking frame without disturbing her. The cat would often curl up inside the space between Mogs's front and back legs, forming a tidy set of shapes—Mogs's legs encircling the cat, and the cat's legs encircling her beloved tennis ball. Mogs clearly accepted the arrangement, so much so one would surmise she appreciated its symmetry, as a philosopher appreciates mathematics without needing to understand its mundane detail.

When Mogs settled into her final resting place in the land where she once roamed, her cohabitants planted a tree next to her grave. It yielded a beautiful blossom and a sharp fruit. I often meditate under that tree.

BRIAN STAFF was born in England, has traveled throughout much of the world, and now lives in Morgan Hill, California. His work ranges from nonfiction to semifiction (marketing materials) to pure fiction (more marketing materials, short stories, and novels). His work has been published in magazines, from technical to literary, and is generally focused on pointing out the absurdities of this thing we call "life." More of his works can be found at *www.wordisworth.com*.

Gibraltar Awash in a Sea of Class Clowns

ROXANNE HAWN

When Lilly and I arrived at our first obedience class, she refused to get out of the car. I cajoled. I tugged. I begged, until she poured to the ground like overcooked linguini. Once there, she flung herself flat, as if a powerful magnet held her in place. I cheered each movement while she snaked toward the door, belly flush to asphalt, refusing my attempts to coax her inside.

When Lilly landed over the threshold after one particularly vigorous flail, I pulled the door closed in victory. That's when I realized everyone was staring. Everyone—people, dogs, the trainer I had not met—watched in silence, goldfish faces gaping. Through giant windows, they'd seen our entire tableau.

Pink-cheeked, I looked for an empty spot, but Lilly found a gap first and flew toward it, dragging me behind her. Oh, she finally wanted to move—but only to hide under a chair. There she cowered, breathing heavily, baring her teeth at anything that moved.

Yep, we were going to be popular.

The trainer patrolled the room as he lectured about teaching us, the people, not our dogs. We needed to learn. We needed to teach. We needed to train. "Communication, not leashes," he warned, "gives you control over your dog."

The message came through: If my words and demeanor made sense to her, she would respond.

After asking a series of questions, the trainer predicted that Lilly would be tops in the class, despite our dramatic entry. I felt dubious. My fellow classmates sat there, amused beyond measure.

Trainer-Man, however, proved himself right. Lilly, a border collie, came as a revelation after the fourteen years I spent with an ornery Dalmatian. Lilly listened to me. She wanted to do what's right. She cared what I thought. But fear, not disobedience, drove her.

I needed to find a way to break through the panic.

I gave Lilly space from the other pups to avoid growls, flashes of teeth, and stink eye. Working border collies control sheep with hard stares and visual fixation. Instinct runs deep. My bossy girl sought control over the other dogs basically by giving them dirty looks.

With a buffer zone and endless food rewards and praise for focusing on me, Lilly shined. She loved learning new things. She bugged me each day—dancing near her leash, squealing with excitement—until I relented and trained her. We worked hard at home with no one watching. Through positive reinforcement, we found a common language and confidence.

Week after week in class, Lilly performed each task as if she were born knowing how. One Saturday, with all twenty dogs in down-stays across the room, the trainer taunted them with noisy toys as he circled the room. Lilly didn't budge. Even when he waved a squawking, shrieking, moaning rubber chicken, my sound-sensitive girl held strong.

Then, Sailor, a big-footed yellow Lab, ripe with puppy fat and unspent energy, lost it. He simply could not stay one . . . more . . . second. As if the floor somehow shook him loose, Sailor leapt to his feet and zoomed around the room, ricocheting off walls, chairs, and people. His invitation to play proved irresistible to the other pups, setting off a chain reaction of broken stays. Chaos reigned.

Lilly observed the scene, never breaking her stay, despite the other pups exploding like rivets from a ship's hull under pressure. Pop . . . golden retriever. Pop . . . black Lab. Pop . . . sheltie.

A Rock of Gibraltar in a sea of motion, Lilly stayed—even while Sailor soaked her with sloppy kisses from tip to tail.

There sat my Einstein in a room full of class clowns.

A few weeks later, the trainer arranged our final exam like a car rally. We took turns heeling our dogs through a course. Various stops required different maneuvers—sit, down, standing-stay. We heeled quickly and slowly; made right turns and left turns; stopped and started in unison.

The exam also required long, group sit-stays and down-stays, as well as at least one individual trick. The trainer awarded ribbons for all that passed, but I knew Lilly had a shot at the top spot and a real trophy. The only other dog with winning potential, a German shepherd, struggled in the exam format and blew off several commands due to nerves. It could easily happen to us, but I held on to hope.

Lilly scored 196 out of 200, beating her closest competitor by at least ten points. Nearly flawless.

Her crowning moment: The stand-for-exam exercise, where the dog remains still while a stranger touches her head, body, feet, and tail. It's a tough task for fearful dogs. Despite my own jitters, I said "Freeze," used our hand signal for a stand-stay, and walked away without doubt or hesitation. Lilly didn't move a muscle.

In the dead-silent room, someone gasped. Not a flinch. Not a wobble. Not one iota of fear. Lilly stood. The same people who once watched us in amusement now sat in awe, as I fought back tears.

The trainer called that goofy yellow Lab into the ring next. I'll never forget his mother's voice as she headed to the start line, "Oh, great! We get to follow Lilly."

The room erupted with laughter.

Not only did I know that we'd won, but also I knew we'd gained so much more. Those eight weeks of basic training created the foundation of our bond, which grows each day. On a Saturday all those years ago, Lilly proved one thing: Beneath her fearful exterior beats the heart of a champion.

ROXANNE HAWN is a full-time freelance writer in Colorado. Her publishing credits include the *New York Times*, *Reader's Digest*, and many other regional and national publications, including several dog magazines. She also chronicles her life with Lilly, her fearful, brilliant, sensitive border collie, through a blog called Champion of My Heart (*www.championofmy heart.com*).

The Country Squire

LUCILLE BELLUCCI

The house we rented in Brazil for a year came with a dog. The landlady had only said, "Don't worry about feeding him." My husband and I thought this strange, but we did not dwell on it. We had much to do in settling in. Curitiba is a small town 3,000 feet above sea level in the south of Brazil; our new home was in a semirural area and had a pear orchard in the back. We met Totó that night, in a manner of speaking. He barked for hours under our bedroom window. We tried telling him to shush and threw some rolled-up comic-strip projectiles in his direction, which worked about as well as they do in, well, comic strips.

In the morning, weary from fragmented sleep, I opened the kitchen door and found Totó seated quietly on the mat. Our tormentor was a mutt, perhaps part German shepherd, a bit runty. His right eye was clouded. I talked to him, telling him the noise had to stop, that finding a dog pound in Curitiba might be a challenge, but I didn't doubt that I would succeed.

He stood up, head inclined, appearing to listen attentively. When the lecture ended, he placed one paw on my foot and licked my ankle. I felt a premonitory pang of weakness. But I quelled it; the night to come would decide if he stayed or went.

Thereon, our slumber remained uninterrupted.

Totó lacked a dog's territorial instinct whenever other animals intruded in our backyard. A capybara, the largest rodent in the world, a powerful animal with fat haunches, was ignored. It was at least four feet long and easily reached into our fruit trees. Capybaras are a food source for Indians, but this one seemed to know I was no Indian and calmly devoured our pears. Totó merely observed, yawning from time to time. When a peccary (a 40- to 50-pound animal resembling a pig with tusks) trotted in one day, Totó hardly glanced in its direction.

Two holes under our fence yielded more traffic than passed through downtown Curitiba. Chickens and ducks browsed in our yard; so did puppies and kittens. Adult dogs and cats did not. I supposed Totó had laid down some kind of rule about that. He stepped carefully around the ducklings and let them guzzle in his water dish, a practice I thought unsanitary. Could they give each other a disease?

I learned why I didn't have to worry about his mealtimes. He sampled the fare at every other house along our block. Everywhere we went together he was greeted by name. A lick on the knee, usually female, served as his hello. Through him I met our neighbors, his meal tickets. They told me that Totó's bad eye was caused by glaucoma.

Sometimes his faithful company caused problems. I tried tying him to a telephone pole outside grocery stores; invariably he would bark and choke himself, coughing, against my bathrobe belt. He didn't wear a collar; most of the country dogs there don't. Finally I was allowed to take him inside the store, where he sat peacefully, giving my knee a lick every so often while I shopped. I noticed then that the burlap sacks of sugar piled at my hip were tilting; they began to sink. Simultaneously, the shopkeeper and I looked down. His leg cocked, Totó was demolishing the bags of sugar. Soon, the remains of fifty pounds of sugar rested in a brown puddle.

The shopkeeper displayed remarkable restraint. I opened my handbag and looked at him. He named a sum. I paid up, and Totó and I slunk out.

Totó hated for me to go out without him. Locked in the kitchen, his cries followed me for blocks. Once, I left him gnawing away on a gristly bone on the front porch and tiptoed around the back to the side gate. At the corner, I boarded a bus headed downtown, paid my fare, and sat down. Then I caught sight of a small figure galloping after the bus, tongue streaming, stride stretched to the limit and beginning to falter. I got off at the next stop.

We went to town together. Our walk started at a comfortable pace, but as we neared town, Totó and I began to have problems staying together. Unaccustomed to sidewalk crowds and troubled by his blind side, he bumped into unknown legs, followed the wrong people. We entered the Loja Americana, a Brazilian version of Woolworth's. After about a minute, I looked around for Totó. No dog. I went outside, rushed up and down the street searching. I spotted him following a woman, fiercely concentrating with his one good eye. I called; his head whipped around. He barked and came careening back to me.

I begged a taxi driver to allow my dog into his car. Exhausted, Totó fell asleep at my feet.

In his own domain, Totó knew what was what. We were experiencing our first Brazilian winter in July. In the state of Paraná, whose northern region crosses the Tropic of Capricorn, temperatures drop to zero. Every night we slung a blanket over the large cage housing our collection of native songbirds. I noticed Totó eyeing the blanket.

One morning I found the birds huddled in a corner of the cage fluffed against the cold like little round powder puffs. Totó snored within the folds of the blanket on the floor.

I bought him a blanket of his own. A fast learner, he commandeered a cushion from the living room. Equipped with pillow and blanket, he became busy at bedtime. He dragged the pillow to a corner, came back for the blanket, and then struggled to adjust his bedding until he was fully satisfied. I am sure he wished he had fingers.

We experienced fogs as total whiteouts. While taking out the garbage one night, feeling my way along the wall, I heard a muffled thudding. It came closer. I froze, and Totó growled and shoved ahead of me. My heart nearly exploded when a huge, long object loomed in front. A horse's head! Totó's growls turned into yips of relief much like my own shaky laughter.

When our year was over, I tried to figure ways we could take him home with us. We knew it was risky taking him out of his natural habitat. He was no longer young, and I could not imagine Totó, the boulevardier of Curitiba's country lanes, tethered to a leash on city streets. The landlady said we could have him if we wished, but she promised he would continue to thrive without us.

We went away without him, convinced that when he ended his days, he would do so on someone's best quilt in a warm house.

LUCILLE BELLUCCI was born in Shanghai, China, and has lived in Italy and Brazil. Her publication credits include short stories, essays, humor/satire, poetry in literary journals and national periodicals such as *Sport Fishing, the new renaissance,* and *Yellow Silk.* Her website is *www.lucillebellucci.com.*

Tribute to Katy

JUDITH GILLE

The end of November 2006 was a wild ride in Seattle, a sort of bite-size Katrina experience. For me, the violent storms, power outages, and subsequent weeks of chaos served mainly as a backdrop for the final act of my thirteen-year-old golden retriever's life. While the wind and rains raged outside, I was sending S.O.S. signals to my veterinarian, searching for advice that would extend my ailing dog's life. Unfortunately, her suggestions yielded no positive change in Katy's condition. My dog's failing kidneys had finally caught up with her. Pummeled by the tempest inside of me, I was forced to acknowledge that it was time to let her go.

Two weeks later, driving home from the veterinarian's office, I was struck by a thought: How could a life force, so full of energy and taking up such a large space in my heart, be reduced to this small, neatly sealed box of ashes by my side?

I pulled over and stared, through tears, at the box. I wished Katy could know how much I missed her. Losing the one creature in the world that loves you best is something many of us will experience at least once—especially anyone who opens his or her home to a canine companion.

The amazing thing about (most) dogs is that they possess all of the best qualities to which we humans aspire. Good dogs are forgiving, loyal, kind, sensitive, nonjudgmental, and protective. Who in your life loves you so unconditionally, always thinks the best of you, and greets you with abundant enthusiasm every time he or she sees you?

I once saw a quote on a refrigerator magnet that said, "Be the kind of person your dog thinks you are." I noted that it didn't say, "Be the kind of person your spouse thinks you are." That might backfire.

Still, a dog, like a spouse, can be a pain in the butt at times. I haven't forgotten the early days when Katy, driven by her puppy energy and anxiety, ripped the sheetrock off the kitchen walls and clawed deep grooves in all the doors. Once she wreaked havoc on the backyard, devastating it in a way I had imagined only some terrible act of nature could. That first year I threatened to give her away numerous times.

But years passed, we survived puppyhood, and I discovered that even the best dogs are slovenly (they never clean up after themselves), inconsiderate (does yours let you sleep in on weekends?) and greedy (sweet Katy would have taken someone's hand off for a T-bone steak).

I learned to accept these personality defects in my dog, and she learned to accept mine and became one of the few steadfast things in my frantically busy life. She greeted me with her whole-body wags and sloppy dog grins when I dashed in the door, and she looked longingly as I hurried out again.

And I have reason to believe that Katy was as reluctant to leave us as we were to let her go. When the vet arrived at our house to put her to sleep, my family and I gathered close. I lit candles and held my ailing dog in my arms for a long time, whispering to her my best wishes for the next life until she had passed. Though the vet took the body when it was over, I left the candles to burn late into the night. When I decided it was time for bed, I carefully blew each one out. Sitting there in the dark, I was certain I felt her presence still in the room.

The next day, I awoke early and stumbled downstairs in the darkness of the early morning to feed the cat. Glancing at Katy's empty bed, I noticed a single candle still burning near it. Though reduced to a mere wick in a puddle of wax, it had relit itself and continued to burn through the night.

When the flicker of life begins to leave our furry friends, we inevitably yearn for more time with them. Remembering the beseeching look in Katy's eyes every time I left her, I only wish I had tried a little harder to be the kind of person she thought I was.

JUDITH GILLE lives in Seattle with her husband and two children. She is currently working on a memoir about her Mexican travels and training the family's newest member—a one-year-old husky-Lab troublemaker named Max. She also had a story published in *My Mom Is My Hero*.

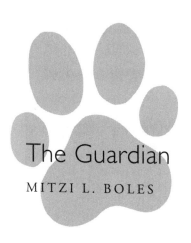

The Guardian

MITZI L. BOLES

"Jeeves, you big lug, get off me!" I grumbled, putting both of my hands on our 150-pound "baby" and trying, unsuccessfully, to shove him back onto the floor. He insisted on being a lapdog, even though his front legs still supported his upper half when he plopped his rump down on my lap, blocking my view of everything in front of me. Named after P.G. Wodehouse's genius gentlemen's gentleman who knew all the answers, our friendly canine hardly lived up to the character's reputation. Our Jeeves was scarcely a gentleman and was far less than brilliant, but he was *our* lovable gentle-giant.

Twenty years earlier, I had vowed never to have another dog in my life. I had handpicked Warlock from a sheepdog-and-Newfoundland-mix litter and spent more than ten wonderful years growing up with the best playmate a lonesome country girl could ever have. Then, quite unexpectedly, Warlock was stolen by someone who accused my family of stealing him as a puppy—even though he had come from my aunt's litter. We ended up in a famous small-town court battle, and we won the case after an ugly trial. Unfortunately, Warlock came home thin and despondent. He didn't hang on much longer.

"You sure you don't regret this?" My husband asked, noticing my tears the day we brought our new puppy home. "Is it bringing back too many memories about Warlock?"

"Uhhh, yeah," I answered, wiping the tears from my eyes. "But look how good Jeeves is with Haley." We studied our big, slobbering pup, now taking up half the living room floor, looking very content, while our daughter bounced on his back, as if he were a galloping pony.

Everyone thought we had been crazy to get a puppy two weeks before Haley was born, but we had our reasons. We wanted a watchdog to guard our family—and Daisy, a young deer I had rescued six months earlier, after a car had struck her. The fawn's chances for survival had been slim, but she had miraculously recovered. As Daisy began maturing into a beautiful young doe, we could no longer contain her in a pen at night. The presence of predatory enemies, lurking in the surrounding dark forest abyss, kept us tossing and turning at night. When I heard about a mixed breed of Anatolian shepherd and Great Pyrenees puppies in town, I thought we'd found a match made in heaven. Farmers in Africa used Anatolians to guard their livestock, so surely one could guard our defenseless fawn against woodland predators.

Jeeves adjusted well to his new home and immediately bonded with Daisy; he slept near her at night and annoyed her during the day. People from all over our rustic community came to watch the doe and her dynamic watchdog at play.

At six months old, Jeeves weighed more than seventy pounds and was nearly equal in size to his hoofed friend. He was so big it was difficult at times to remember that he was a puppy and to forgive him for his many transgressions. He chewed everything—and everyone. I had my hands full with Haley, but in between diaper changes, Jeeves and I worked on disciplinary skills. I managed to save a few garden hoses, along with other prohibited paraphernalia, from being dragged to the special spot on the lawn where he demolished things. He often reminded me of Warlock, as if life had come full circle, and I had finally found my way back to country living with a treasured canine friend. When I observed Jeeves herding my spirited child away from climbing the fence, I realized how blessed we were to have him as our watchdog.

One warm summer evening, as Matt and I lay in bed listening to coyotes baying at the full moon, Jeeves suddenly began barking loudly and uncontrollably. Matt and I ran outside, only to hear a clanging sound echo off the fence. Once we calmed Jeeves, we praised him for scaring off whatever was out there.

The next morning we realized Daisy was missing. She must have become frightened and jumped the fence. Sick with worry, we hiked the forest trails and drove around for miles looking for her. Alas, our mission failed, and we headed home. We worried about our little fawn facing the perils of the surrounding woods and nearby highway. Her only hope lay in uniting with one of the migrating deer herds, which was the ultimate plan, when she was ready—but she wasn't ready.

Before sunrise another succession of loud barks awakened me. As I opened the front gate to investigate the nature of Jeeves's distress, he pushed past me and ran, at full gallop, toward the woods. I tried running after him, but before I knew it, the vast forest of ponderosa pine had swallowed him up. Now two of my precious babies were missing!

After awakening Matt, I set out for the trails, and then saw something I couldn't believe: Two figures emerged from the woods, slowly trotting toward our home. One was the big, fluffy white blob known as Jeeves, and tramping steps ahead of him, being herded along, was a very weary-looking yearling. Daisy appeared cut, bruised, and exhausted—yet very much safe and alive. Jeeves had shepherded her home and proved himself to be the best dog any family, or lonesome deer, could ever have.

MITZI L. BOLES lives in Payson, Arizona, with her husband and daughter. She has a BA in Journalism and is a state-licensed wildlife rehabilitator. Her goal as a writer and rehabilitator is to encourage respect and empathy for nature by raising awareness about the environment and the animals that inhabit it. Mitzi also had a story published in *My Teacher Is My Hero*. Mitzi's work can be found at *www.wondersofthewild.org*.

On Tour with the Ambassador

GARY PRESLEY

"Don't you think greyhound dogs are elegant?" my wife asked. "If we had one, I could take it jogging with me."

You can see the Yupster was her idea. I remained leery. I thought adopting a retired racing greyhound—my spouse's ticket to good health via good deeds—might mean we'd end up with a dog both hyper and hard to handle.

I had had all sorts of dogs in my life, but what I knew about greyhounds could have been etched on a dog collar nameplate. Nevertheless, I considered myself wise in the ways of marriage; I understood that the men most happily married are those who regularly respond, "Sure, baby, whatever you want." And so we set out to equip the woman of my dreams with jogging necessities: trendy running shoes, nifty matching sweatbands, and a greyhound dog.

We easily found a local representative of the Greyhound Pets of America, a group dedicated to finding homes for greyhounds no longer competitive on the racetrack. After filling out a form, attending an approval meeting, and paying a small fee, we found ourselves sharing our home with Sportin' Yuppie, a three-year-old retired racing greyhound.

Unfortunately, three months into our *Adventures in Greyhoundland*, a detour occurred: My wife broke her right ankle—no, not jogging, stepping off a stool. Yuppie had nothing to do with it. As the doctor finished strapping on my wife's walking cast, he said, "That's the end of your jogging days for a while, young lady."

"What he means," my lovely wife said, "is that you need more fresh air, Gary."

So that's how I ended up sitting at the end of my driveway with a greyhound tied to the end of my arm, eager to reel off a couple of miles on the streets of our small town. I looked down at my power wheelchair, and then at Yuppie—a big, shiny black creature made up mostly of legs and tail and snout, a dog who draws attention wherever he goes—and sighed. A man who could not walk had been relegated to making the social scene with a dog born to race and only recently retired. *Someone* has a sense of humor, I thought, before taking a deep breath and setting out to justify my existence in the greyhound scheme of life.

I learned quickly that Yuppie would always be ready for a walk. The big fellow was patient and obedient when on his leash, but he would begin to tug if he saw rapid movement—say, a squirrel, or most exciting, a barking dog riding in the back of a pickup. When that occurred on our very first adventure, Yuppie took off like he actually understood what "racing" meant. He passed the truck in midblock and waited patiently at the next stop sign to express his displeasure at the cheating dog riding in the truck bed.

I was glad I let go. I wouldn't have wanted to slow him down bouncing along at the end of the leash. That incident, however, made me theorize that the Yupster had rigged a con game to get out of racing. I could almost hear him whispering to the hounds in the kennel, *Hey, guys, I hear if you throw a few races there's a good chance a cushy early retirement is in your future.*

Somewhere along the line, Yuppie had missed the part about all adopted greyhounds being neutered. This dichotomy might have explained his perpetually goofy smile, i.e., elegant racing dogs may not be the brightest dogs on the block.

In fact, without maligning the breed, Yuppie was a lovable doofus, one whose priorities in life were worshiping my wife and pursuing regular meals and snacks. Visualize a seventy-five-pound solid black dog—and the neat, organized house where he lived—who has managed to climb a shelf to find and rip open a box of pancake mix to help tide him over until dinner. Need I say "flour, flour everywhere?"

Yuppie had one other diabolical love—ear rubs. If anyone innocently began rubbing his ears, he would respond by leaning amorously against the legs of the person doing the rubbing and groaning so enthusiastically, so passionately that shy people would often blush and run from the room.

But mostly Yuppie slept—eighteen hours a day on his personal afghan rug, which he carried from room to room. He soon became a peaceful, gentle companion snoring softly and sometimes whimpering as he sped across some imaginary open ground where there were no leashes and no kennels. As the adoption people liked to say, "Greyhounds are 40-mph couch potatoes."

I walked the Yupster at least once or twice a day for more than ten years, and invariably whenever I met anyone new they always asked, "What kind of dog is that anyway?"

And not a day passed that I didn't want to answer, "It's my seeing leg dog." But I didn't. I knew my obligation in this strange partnership was to work as assistant to Yuppie, who seemed to have elected himself the local adoption ambassador. Few dogs make better companions than greyhounds, and so Yuppie and I would go calmly about our daily goodwill tour on behalf of retired racers everywhere, him smiling amiably, me working the crowd with my spiel.

"Yes," I would say, smiling, "They make great pets."

"Yes, they are quiet, clean, and friendly."

"Actually, they're not hyper."

"There's an organized effort to adopt out retired racers. I can give you the 800 number, if you'd like."

And thus Yuppie and I toured our neighborhood, year upon year, marking our travels along the streets by the progression of irate barking dogs we encountered along our route. I must say Yuppie was one cool customer. He would never look at them, never show any fear, and never bark in response to the 400-watt canine woofers, even if they were pit bulls, Dobermans, or Rottweilers. I always had the feeling Yuppie dismissed them easily, thinking, *OK, jump the fence, loudmouth. All you're going to see are my taillights.*

What would have happened to me if one of those ill-tempered louts had come bolting over the fence? If I know Yuppie (and I think I do), he would have weighed the outcome in a split second by thinking about his afghan rug, his next meal, and an affectionate ear rub from my wife.

But I think he would have remembered me fondly—eventually.

GARY PRESLEY has written for publications as diverse as Salon. com and *Notre Dame Magazine*. The University of Iowa Press published Gary's memoir, *Seven Wheelchairs: A Life Beyond Polio*, in 2008. Reach Presley through his website: *www.garypresley.com*.

Turbo, Our Extraordinary Canine Hero

ED KOSTRO

"If I have any beliefs about immortality,
Certain dogs that I have known will go to Heaven,
And very few persons will."
—James Thurber

I've been extremely blessed throughout my lifetime to have known and lived with many great dogs; and now, my wife and I have one that I believe is truly extraordinary.

Turbo hails from the Navajo Indian Nation in New Mexico, where he began life as a stray, an unwanted "rez dog." But luckily, a most kind-hearted Native American woman rescued him, along with many other homeless canines on the reservation, and I was fortunate enough to be the one who adopted him.

My veterinarian identified Turbo as part cattle dog, part German shepherd, and maybe, even part Mexican wolf. I say he's also part angel. Turbo is a large, muscular, black dog that can be as fierce as a wolf but also as gentle as a lamb. Though he towers over her, he absolutely adores our little female Chihuahua. He's also one of the most intelligent dogs I've ever had, one of the most courageous, and one of the most compassionate. And he thinks he's a musician (but more about that later).

Turbo also serves as our extremely diligent guardian and protector. He would gladly give his life protecting any of us: human, canine, or feline. When our twenty-year-old cat, Buddy, suddenly took ill, Turbo refused to leave his side, smothering him with wet kisses and doing his best to comfort him. He would watch over old Buddy like a hawk, gently guiding him up and down stairways and diligently standing over him while he ate so none of our other animals could bother him. When Buddy napped in the sun, Turbo stayed right by his side. And when Buddy so sadly passed on, Turbo took it hard, suffering miserably for several weeks.

Compassionate Turbo now very diligently watches over me when I'm working around the house on maintenance projects. This summer, I fell off a ladder, bouncing my head on a concrete slab. Luckily, I have a very thick skull; but as I was sprawled on the ground in a slight daze, Turbo grabbed me by the shirt collar and vehemently tugged me toward the shade, out of the broiling sun's rays. He must have instinctively known that I wasn't hurt very badly, because as soon as he made sure I wouldn't fry in the hot sun, he raced off to jump in the cool, refreshing kiddie pool with his canine pal, Tater.

Besides being our protector and nursemaid, Turbo considers himself a grand musician. He absolutely loves squeak toys of all shapes and sizes. He seems to sense when I've brought a new one home, as he dashes in to excitedly stick his nose into each and every shopping bag until he finds his new treasure; and then he races off with it in his mouth, a huge canine grin on his face.

And every time that I call out, "Play us a tune, Turbo!" he starts squeaking that toy like there's no tomorrow—and he's actually pretty good at it. We think his methodic squeaks have a definite musical quality to them.

But our aspiring canine musician has one big problem—each and every time Turbo puts down his latest glorious musical toy, even for a minute, our dog Junior will rush in, grab it, and very quickly rip it to shreds, searching for the hidden plastic squeak mechanism inside. And each and every time that Junior destroys his latest cherished musical toy, Turbo will bring it to me, drop it in my hand, and look at me very glumly, as if to say, "It's broken; can you fix it, please?" And, of course, I always get him a new one.

A few months ago, violent thunderstorms, one after the other, accompanied by 60- to 70-mph winds, pummeled the entire Midwest. Soon, uprooted trees and downed power lines were everywhere. Toward evening, during a break in the violent storm activity, I let all four of our dogs out into the yard. Within seconds, Turbo picked something up and raced back to me. I knelt down, opened my hand, and Turbo deposited an infant sparrow into my palm. The tiny baby must have been blown out of its nest in the storm, but luckily it was still breathing. Turbo looked at me as if saying, "Can you fix it, please?"

We rushed the little sparrow inside the house, warmed it, wrapped it in a towel, and placed it in a box. And of course, Turbo diligently stood guard over that small cardboard box throughout the evening. He wouldn't let any of our other dogs or cats near it. Unfortunately, I knew the infant bird had a very slim chance of survival. It desperately needed its mother, and the likelihood that I would find her nest in the dark was nil. The best we could do was keep it warm and dry, and wait for morning.

During the night our very compassionate and heroic canine nursemaid let out a long, mournful sigh, and I knew the bird had died. When I buried the tiny sparrow the next morning, a very glum-looking Turbo stood right by my side.

ED KOSTRO is a published freelance writer, book author, and animal advocate. His work has appeared in *Chicken Soup for the Dog Lover's Soul, Cats Do It Better Than People, Pets: Part of the Family, PetLife,* and *Catholic Digest.* His latest book, *Through Katrina's Eyes, Poems from an Animal Rescuer's Soul,* depicts some of the stories of the many remarkable animals and humans he met during this nation's largest pet rescue endeavor on America's Gulf Coast.

The Amazing Boodini

JAMES E. SCHMID, JR.

When I was ten years old, my mother announced that our family needed a dog; and not just any dog, a Yorkshire terrier. At the pet store, five small puppies were climbing all over each other, trying to play in a three-foot-square cage amid billowing newspaper scraps. We selected the friskiest of the little black lumps and named him Boo-boo.

After a few weeks, the black ball of fur grew into a large feather duster with four skinny feet, a brown face and a large, brown walruslike beard. Little did we realize we were staring at the face of the greatest dog escape artist ever to walk the earth.

For the first two weeks, Boo-boo lived in the living room, but when he began to get into mischief, my parents decided to banish our frisky puppy to the basement at night. My father bought wood and wire fencing and spent the better part of a Sunday building a pen in a corner of our basement. When introduced to his new bedroom, Boo-boo announced his displeasure so loudly and long, the whole neighborhood could hear. As my father turned to go back upstairs, our mischievous puppy suddenly stopped barking. My father smiled, assuming Boo-boo was getting used to the pen. Two seconds later, he felt a quick swoosh of air pass his leg. By the time Dad lifted his head, Boo-boo was sitting at the top of the stairs, tongue out and stubby tail wagging, fully expecting to be congratulated for passing the test. Apparently, Boo-boo couldn't bark and climb the three-foot fence at the same time.

My father went back downstairs, added another foot to the pen, and once again placed the little one-foot-high pup inside. Once again, tremendous barking suddenly stopped, but this time my father swung around to find that the dog was actually jumping up and catching the top of the fence with his front paws and pulling himself over. It was apparent that Boo-boo was going to win this round, as he beat Dad up the stairs again.

Round three commenced the following day when my father, not wanting to be outdone, purchased a pet taxi. After he placed Boo-boo in it that night, barking, scratching, and loud protestation occurred, per usual . . . and then silence. My father, feeling smug, smiled. Little did he know that Boo-boo had quit scratching and barking because he had managed to unseat the four screws in the back of the cage and force himself between the top and side of the taxi to escape once again. After investigating the basement for a few minutes, Boo-boo ascended the stairs and announced his victory by scratching loudly and long at the basement door. I swear that little brown-faced dog shot my father a naïve silly grin as if to say, *Next.* My father couldn't believe it. He shook his head, gave up for the night, and we all went to bed.

The next day, my father made a second trip to the pet store and brought home a metal cage for the escape artist. The bars on this cage were about as thick as a small ballpoint pen and spaced tightly. When my father opened the door of the cage and placed the offender in, he felt certain he had conquered his rival this time. Boo-boo must have wised up, because this time he did not announce his victory until the next morning. When my father opened the basement door, Boo-boo pranced out, wagging his tail, and, adding insult to injury, jumped onto my father's recliner. He looked at my chagrined father as if to say, *Go on down there and try to build something that can hold me captive . . . I double-dog dare you.* A close inspection revealed that Boo-boo had climbed to the top of the four-foot cage and managed not only to bend the wire on the cage, but also to break two or three wires to create an exit. This dog was determined to maintain his freedom.

That day, my father constructed a Boo-boo-proof cage by wrapping heavy-gauge chicken wire around the metal cage. When he cautiously opened the door the next morning and Boo-boo was not there to meet him, the look of utter relief on my father's face was priceless. He had finally managed to keep the small yet very wily dog in the cage for an entire night. That night and the next few nights, however, Boo-boo resorted to emotional appeals. He would howl and cry until one of my parents would finally give up, release him, and take him upstairs.

Boo-boo's escape ability transcended to legend when the family went on vacation to Florida. Boo-boo was sentenced to stay in a kennel for an entire week while we made our annual pilgrimage to the beach. When we returned, we found Boo-boo huddled up in a portion of the kennel normally reserved for cats. When my father asked what had happened, the kennel manager reported that Boo-boo had scaled a seven-foot fence and had escaped from his normal cage. The only way they could keep him locked up was to use the cages set aside for the cats. My parents decided then and there that Boo-boo loved his freedom so much that no one should ever confine him to a cage.

My father and Boo-boo became inseparable. I cannot remember a time after that incident that he was not curled up in my father's lap on the recliner or sitting on his feet as he read a book. When Boo-boo passed away, my father wept as if his child had died. Boo-boo was awarded full funeral rights. A well-kept grave marker, on the hill in my parents' yard, marks where he was laid to rest. It honors an extraordinary dog, the *Amazing Boodini.*

JAMES E. SCHMID, JR. is a freelance writer who has developed everything from web copy to short stories. He has been a dog owner since he was a small child. Even though he has had many types of dogs, he will never find one to replace Boo-boo the great escape artist.

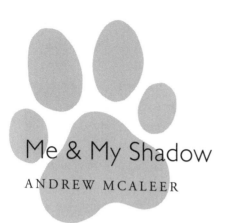

Me & My Shadow

ANDREW MCALEER

From the moment I saw her, in a humane society cage, I sensed something special about Shadow. While still a puppy, Shadow had lost her right foreleg in a car accident, and the volunteers had attached a card to her cage that read: "I'm Shadow, I'm four and half, and I only have three legs, but I still love to run and play." A black Lab mix, she had been admitted five months earlier by her owners, and I could tell she had been caged too long. I decided to take her for a trial walk to boost her spirits.

On the walk, despite having only three legs, Shadow bounced from flower to flower, shrub to shrub, drainpipe to drainpipe, pulling hard, as if she were a lead sled dog. I couldn't bear the idea of returning her to a caged existence. I signed for the adoption and happily lifted Shadow into my truck, making this the first of thousands of times I would lift her.

Shadow didn't view herself as crippled. The first time I took her to the beach, she leapt into the water and vigorously chased drifting seagulls, so vigorously I was afraid she would tire herself out and I waded out to escort her back to shore. When the local kids played street hockey, Shadow swiped many a ball—raising her back like a slinky and pogoing her front leg as she made her escape. Clearly, Shadow loved those kids: She rushed out in the mornings to play with them at the bus stop and waited anxiously to greet them when they dropped by after school.

Shadow made friends easily, but she made a few enemies, too. One day, as I was mowing the lawn, Shadow discovered an underground bees' nest, rooted around it, and soon came scurrying over to take cover between my legs. When the bees surrounded us and started to attack me, I scooped Shadow up and hotfooted us to safety. Shadow recovered from the trauma and was soon sleeping peacefully on my bed. I didn't have the heart to awaken her, so I resumed mowing solo.

Shadow had become a valued companion, but I had no idea how much she meant to me until a dark day in October 1999. It began as our usual Sunday in the park, but it screeched toward disaster when Shadow leapt out of the truck and ran across the street toward another dog. Just then, a car careened around the corner and struck Shadow, tossing her about thirty feet onto the curb. I dashed over to her, gingerly lifted her, lay her on the seat beside me, and raced to the vet. After an examination, the doctor delivered the good news: She had not sustained any damage to her organs. And then the bad news: Her back-left femur had been fractured in ten places. About that time, I heard Shadow barking from her cage, calling me. When I entered the room, she pulled herself up on her two good legs and cried for help. I asked the doctor to sedate her for the night so that I could take her to a specialized facility the next day.

The next day, Shadow survived an eight-hour operation during which the bone specialist wired her shattered bones together and screwed a metal plate into the remaining chunks of bone at her sockets. He had to use more than sixty staples to secure the wound. Even though she had to stay in the dog hospital eleven days, Shadow displayed her trademark determination and never gave up.

Shadow's recovery was slow, and she wasn't always patient. She had been home only a few weeks when I carried her outside for some sun. Since she couldn't walk yet, I went back inside to retrieve a book. When I returned, the patient was gone! I ran around to the other side of the yard, where I found Shadow toe-touching on her traumatized leg. Worried that she would reopen the wounds, I put my hands under her to help her walk. For the next few months, Shadow found other ways to stabilize her wobbly body. While conducting business, she would lean against the magnolia tree, buttress herself in the pachysandra, and extend her back leg out as if doing a runner's stretch. With time, a lot of patience, and incredible fortitude, Shadow eventually recovered almost full use of her leg.

Shadow's indomitable spirit not only inspired me but also my entire family. When my father's lymphoma worsened, I would often find her either sleeping in his office while he typed or waiting on the front lawn for him. Shadow and my father bonded over food—my father would often stash a box of oversized bones in his car and dole them out to Shadow regularly.

When my mother was diagnosed with fourth-stage breast cancer and quickly declined, Shadow would consistently park herself next to my mother's chair, dozing with a watchful eye that popped open regularly. When we moved my mother's bed into the dining room, Shadow would sleep by her bed night after night.

Shadow proved her loyalty by tending to my parents throughout their illnesses and death, but more trials lay ahead. Shortly after my parents died (within days of each other), I was diagnosed with third-stage melanoma and required immediate surgery. Two days after the procedure, I toe-touched it out of the hospital with a wound running from my inner thigh up to my pelvis.

Well-meaning family and friends expressed concern that I would no longer be able to lift Shadow—or care for her basic needs—and offered to take care of her at their homes. Shadow was almost fifteen years old at the time and could no longer negotiate the stairs nor leap into my bed. Nevertheless, Shadow knew that I needed her, and I knew that she needed me. When she needed a lift, I assured my friends, I would simply find a way to manage.

Two months after my surgery, I faced rounds of interferon that led to nausea and vomiting. For a while, I couldn't take fluids except intravenously; I couldn't eat because of the chronic vomiting. Soon, I could count my bones. My normal fight had subsided, and I often lay limp on my bed. Many well-meaning friends again offered to take Shadow off my hands, but if anyone tried to lure her away, she growled and glued herself to my side.

As my ordeal dragged on, every step of the way, Shadow saved me. To many she looked lazy, curled up at the end of my bed, snuggled up in my father's elbow-worn Pendletons, dreaming of roast beef. To me, she looked like the most loyal companion a man could want. The feel of her frosty snout resting on my bad leg was just the lift I needed. With Shadow's help, I regained my health and enjoyed her companionship for several years to come.

ANDREW MCALEER works for the Massachusetts Department of Corrections. He recently authored *101 Habits of Highly Successful Novelists* and had a story published in *My Dad Is My Hero*. Mr. McAleer is also a specialist with the Army National Guard.

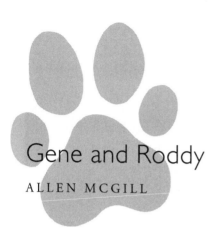

Gene and Roddy

ALLEN MCGILL

Growing up in New York City, I was fortunate to be part of the "small-town" community that Greenwich Village was back then. Long-term residents of one of the city's oldest communities knew each other, tolerated each other, and cared for each other. As with all neighborhoods, especially of the "artistic" persuasion, we had our characters. Gene and Roddy were two who were special to all of us.

Gene was an old man who, in his day, must have been quite the dandy. He was always nattily dressed with jacket and tie, always erect as if on parade, and always ready to tip his hat to a passing lady. He was also always inebriated.

Roddy was his white and tan Jack Russell terrier. He was older than Gene in dog years, friendly, feisty, and in his later years blind. By sense of smell, it was presumed, Roddy recognized everyone who lived on the street who took the time to stop to pet and say hello to him. He returned all such greeting with fingertip kisses.

The two were inseparable. Gene would tuck Roddy under his arm and carry him down the steps from his top-floor apartment in a converted townhouse to the tree-lined street. He'd place him gently beyond the curb near a car wheel so Roddy could sniff out any new visitors to the neighborhood. Gene always managed to do so without falling, no matter how tipsy he was at the time. And Roddy didn't need a leash, since he never strayed more than two feet from Gene's pant legs. They'd been together for years, two old gents relying on each other for love, comfort, and companionship.

One crisp autumn evening, a taxi pulled up in front of the townhouse, and Gene emerged, considerably less able to maneuver than usual. He stumbled out the door, swung it shut behind him, and leaned through the window to pay the fare. He then forced himself upright, and the taxi drove off.

"No, wait!" Gene cried frantically, waving his arms and staggering after the cab. "Roddy!" The cab drove out of sight. Roddy had been in the back seat, momentarily forgotten by Gene.

The news spread quickly that Roddy was missing. Neighborhood residents were thrown into stunned concern. They joined forces to search and call throughout the city in an attempt to find the elderly canine. No one gave voice to the images each of us had of the horrible things that might happen to poor Roddy, an old, blind dog in a city of millions. Every avenue of tracking him down was followed, which included the calling of all known taxi companies, various police precincts and the American Society for the Prevention of Cruelty to Animals—all with no results.

A week passed without Gene leaving the proximity of his telephone. But one night he did appear: unshaven, gaunt, disheveled—and sober. He took to roaming the streets nightly, to search beneath parked cars, peer down basement stairs, and look through store windows. I walked with him, in silence, just so he wouldn't be alone. Another week passed; Gene seemed to grow more and more frail with each passing day.

"Let's sit for a minute," I suggested one night, when we again reached his stoop.

He nodded, and then eased down onto a step, wrapping his arms around himself. After only a few minutes he rose again, saying, "I'm so cold. It's time for me to go," and he turned to wend his way up the long flights of stairs.

"Hey, mister," I heard a man's voice call. "You lose a dog?"

Gene spun around so quickly I was afraid he was going to tumble down the stone steps. "Yes!" he croaked. Hope and disbelief burst forth in the single word.

"Thought I recognized you," the voice called again. A large man stepped out from the driver's seat of an off-duty yellow cab. He reached back inside and drew forth a small dog into his arms. It was Roddy!

With an outcry of laughter mixed with tears, Gene stumbled down to the sidewalk, arms outstretched, unable to speak. Roddy struggled in the cabby's arms and let out a single "Yip!" That was the first and only time I ever heard him bark. The cabby handed him over. Roddy, tail wagging with the vigor of an excited pup, placed both paws on Gene's face to hold him still while he covered every inch of lickable face with kisses.

The man turned to me: "It wasn't until I got home that I discovered the little fella in the back seat of my cab."

"But we called all the taxi companies," I told him. "How come?"

The man shrugged. "I notified headquarters, but it was late. The message must have gotten lost in the shift change. I own my own cab and that was my last call of the night, so afterward I drove home. I was going on vacation the next day, but when I found this little guy I realized the old man must be frantic. I know I would be. So I've been driving around this neighborhood and the one where I picked him up every day for the past two weeks, hoping I might see him. I was giving up after tonight." He glanced at the notice on a nearby tree, and then added, "Guess I should have walked. I couldn't see the 'Lost Dog' fliers from the cab."

"I can't tell you how much this means to me," Gene managed to say, still choked with emotion.

"You don't have to," the cabby said, smiling. He reached out to scratch Roddy under the chin and was rewarded by Roddy nuzzling his face into his palm, adding a few licks for good measure before returning his attention to Gene's nose.

After effusive thanks and offers of a reward—refused by the cabby—each of us went our separate way. Things returned to the way I'd always known them—well, almost. Gene still took Roddy for his evening "constitutionals," but they lasted longer than they had before. Each one now ended at an Alcoholics Anonymous meeting, where Roddy slept in Gene's arms until it was time for them to go home again, together.

Roddy came into my care shortly after . . . but that's another story.

ALLEN MCGILL lives, writes, acts, and directs theater in Mexico. His work has been published in hundreds of online and paper publications, including the *New York Times*. He was a member of PEN, and two of his plays have been professionally produced in Sacramento and Los Angeles, California.

Mozart Must Have Had a Poodle

CASSIE RODGERS

Samantha was her name, but Sammie seemed much more appropriate. And Sammie was never a hero in any traditional sense. She didn't drag a child from a burning building or chase away a potential villain lurking in the long weeds that surrounded our tiny house in the country. Of course she would have tried, if she ever got the chance. She never let her shin's-eye view of the world keep her from looking anyone, or anything, right in the eye. In any case, I doubt anybody would have run. Maybe from our German shepherd, but not from a chubby, hairy, kind of white miniature poodle lacking all of her front teeth. She had lost those teeth bravely on the carpet of battle with her arch nemesis—the vacuum cleaner. She didn't know what it was; perhaps it did have the potential to kill. The Dirt Devil had certainly maimed Sammie. Thus, I too came to fear it and avoided it as if it was a rabid skunk. I knew dogs were much more intuitive than people, so perhaps Sammie was wiser than my parents, at least in regards to cleaning apparatus.

Sammie was my dog from the moment she arrived in my life as a six-week-old puppy, for my seventh birthday, until her death early on in my sophomore year of college. She was thirteen years old and had been having heart troubles for the past few years. I was not home when she had to be put to sleep. When my mom called with the news, I thought I could be a tough, independent woman and discuss the tragic events quietly and calmly.

My mom took a breath and said, "Sammie had to be put to sleep today."

"Oh." I was fighting to keep my resolve.

"Are you okay? Can you talk?"

"Yeah, no, I'm . . ." and my resolve failed, after four words, five, depending on how you feel about contractions. And if expressions like "oh" count as a word and you don't take into account that "yeah" and "no" cancel each other out. Any way you tally it, I was still a girl, and my best friend had died. I cried for several hours, curled up in my lofted dorm bed, much to the discomfort of my roommate, who couldn't hear the news I could not articulate. The next couple of days I tried to focus on my schoolwork, but my sloppy notes turned into careful caricatures of a little poodle with big eyes and a shiny nose.

I made the two-hour trip home that weekend, even though Sammie had already been laid to rest. When I arrived home, nobody was around. I was thankful for the time I would have alone, to talk to the pile of soft, reddish brown dirt under which Sammie was now nestled. When I actually stood over the little mound of dirt in a remote area of our backyard, my bones seemingly dissolved, and I collapsed onto the trampled grass surrounding the unmarked grave.

Actually, the grave was marked. My hand had landed on something cooler than the autumn ground. I opened my sopping-wet eyes and found my hand had come to rest on Sammie's collar, forgotten in the funerary turmoil, when minds and eyes were ensconced in wet, heavy fogs of grief. I clutched it tightly, my eyelids holding my tears in with similar force, until the edges of her bone-shaped ID tag left deep grooves in my hand.

I remembered getting that tag, when Sammie and I were still very young. I had been so proud because my mother had engraved my name in the spot designated for the owner, the person in charge. My parents had laughed at me for staring at it for so long, a goofy, proud smile on my face. My mother had later glued the name tag to Sammie's rabies tag because she couldn't stand the jingle they made when Sammie pranced around the house. I only grudgingly complied, maintaining that Sammie and I enjoyed the music she created. Later, I realized that sound had probably inspired the light dancing step that always seemed to muddle her real age. For Sammie, music became the fountain of youth.

When her tags no longer jingled, Sammie found a plastic mat kept near an outside door that emitted a dull but cheery little tap when she walked across it. Sammie would do a little tap dance on it, walking back and forth in uneven strides that created a happy little patter. Whoever was nearby would unthinkingly open the door and release Sammie into the outdoors. I'm not sure how long she had been doing this before we all realized it was her way of getting our attention. On occasion, she refused to go outside. All she had really wanted was affection.

Because I was the only girl of five children, I thought of Sammie as the sister I longed to have. My brothers often made fun of my little white poodle, but their words never stopped her from standing up for me, snarling while they attempted to tickle or otherwise taunt me, as brothers do. Eventually they, too, grew fond of Sammie and left us alone.

Sammie never saved my life, but she brought music to it—not the typical music played on the radio, but rather an underlying tempo and harmony that made my own song that much stronger. Sammie's song will always play on in me. Heroic dogs don't have to be big, strapping German shepherds, saving babies and stopping bad guys. Sometimes they can be little dogs, with bad publicists and even worse haircuts, who save the world by defeating their enemies—one vacuum cleaner at a time.

CASSIE RODGERS is an aspiring writer making her home in Minnesota. She has a great love of animals and would be in veterinary school now if chemistry weren't so gosh-darn difficult!

A Dog Named Bum

LARRY CONNER

Bum was a purebred pointer. My Uncle Roy would never have any other type of bird dog. Bum was all white except for a brown patch that covered each ear, and he weighed about sixty pounds—the same as me at the time. He always had a quizzical glint in his brown eyes when he looked at me, as if saying: "Come on, what are we going to do next?" My uncle called him Bum because he would rather lie sprawled out in the sunshine than go hunting. Despite three years of effort by my uncle, Bum never successfully pointed a covey of quail. Finally, my uncle gave the dog to me.

I was eight and called the dog Bumzo because I loved him. He answered to either name with the same joyous abandon. "Here Bumzo," I would yell. He would come galloping across the yard; eyes scrunched shut, lips grinning, his tongue lolling out so far, you thought he might trip on it. Usually he would forget to stop when he got to me, and there would be a crash. Big bird dog and little boy would go tumbling across the grass in a big, happy tangle.

One Saturday morning in early April, my daddy decided to take Bum and me on a fishing trip to one of the deep creeks that run through the woods of north Georgia. The rolling foothills that were our destination were not big enough to be called mountains, but it was still very rugged country.

Daddy finally found just the right spot and parked the car beside the dusty red clay road. We grabbed our cane fishing poles and the can of bait and headed for the creek. This was a day to relish. Quail were bobwhiting in the fields, and rabbits and squirrels played in the sunshine. Bum and I could scarcely contain our glee in being out in the country on such a beautiful day. Off to the west, we could see a line of dark thunderclouds slowly building, but they were still too low on the horizon to concern us.

Bum led the way even though he didn't know where we were going. He was sniffing and bumbling along, annoying the squirrels and rabbits, and scattering quail whenever he stumbled on a covey. Bum never did learn to point birds.

Soon we came to the steep banks of the creek we were going to explore. The red clay banks were approximately twenty feet high and so steep that only one small path about two feet wide led down to the shallow but fast-moving water. We were wearing old shoes, so we started walking up the sun-dappled stream, looking for a good fishing hole. Bum was leading the way, scaring the fish the same way he had spooked the quail.

By noon we had walked about two miles up the creek. We hadn't found a really good fishing spot, but we didn't mind. My father and I both loved to walk, so we were having a good time being together in the woods. Bum, being Bum, was happy doing whatever I was doing. The water ran cold around our ankles, a soothing contrast to the hot Georgia sunlight sifting down through the overhanging trees.

There were rumblings of thunder coming from the west now, and although it seemed to be getting louder, it still didn't bother us. All this changed at about one o'clock, when black clouds rolled overhead and the gentle breeze changed to a cold, angry wind. Bum became very agitated and stuck close to my side. Soon the whole sky turned black. First, we felt a light sprinkle that quickly grew in intensity to great globs of icy rain. Lighting slashed into the trees along the top of the bank, the nearly simultaneous claps of thunder stunning our ears.

We wanted to get out of the creek, but we could not find a way up the high, slick banks. Our clothes were soaked, and Bum shivered from the rain pelting his short, white fur. All thoughts of fishing had vanished as we stumbled back through the deepening water toward our car. Water cascaded down the slippery banks of that canyon of a creek bed, adding to the growing flood. We had lost our fishing poles and bait can, but that was the least of our worries. I was having trouble keeping my footing, and Bum was having even more difficulty than me. Sometimes Bum would actually swim to keep his head above the tumbling flood, but he never left my side. The rain continued to fall, the lightning flashed, the thunder boomed, and the water kept moving higher up past my knees.

At last, I saw the path ahead! Soaked to the skin, my teeth chattering, I stumbled toward it, fighting to keep my footing in the rushing waters. Bum treaded water beside me, waiting for me to go up the path first. However, just as I stepped up onto the bank, Bum suddenly pushed me aside and jumped up on the path ahead of me. For a moment I thought: "You Bum of a dog, trying to get out of the water first, ahead of me, your best friend." Then I saw what Bum had already seen. A cottonmouth water moccasin, its evil-black four-foot body, thicker than a man's arm, lay coiled in the path just clear of the water. Like us, it had crawled up onto the path seeking to escape the flood.

Bum must have realized what was happening and moved to shield my body with his own. Then as the snake prepared to strike, Bum reared up, his weight pushing me backward into the water. I heard Bum yelp as the snake sank his fangs into my protector's left front paw. Bum fell into the water beside me, and the snake, figuring things were getting too crowded, slithered away into the underbrush.

By this time Daddy had caught up with us. Picking up Bum, he ran to the car with him. Our veterinarian treated Bum's bite, and in a few days, he was as good as new. Soon we were running across the fields again. Bum never learned to point a covey of quail, but he did save my life.

LARRY CONNER is a retired naval aviator with nearly 6,000 hours of flight time. His writing experience includes news releases and human-interest articles for Navy publications including *Navy Times* and *All Hands Magazines* and four years on the staff of the *Auburn Plainsman*, the Auburn University student newspaper. He recently completed a 95,000-word adventure novel based on his experiences in Africa.

Queen of My Heart

RUTH ANDREW

The year was 1947, and I was six years old when a little black and white English bulldog came to live at our house. Early on, Queenie let me daily plunk her into my white wicker bicycle basket, and she behaved like an angel as we rode to the corner grocery store to buy two loaves of Wonder bread for my mother. In those days, a pet could go into the store with you, at least at our corner grocery store. The owner always gave Queenie a treat, so of course she had to go in with me. She wasn't one to be left behind. I always had to hold the bag of bread in my hand as we rode back home, because the basket on my bike was filled with the dog. As I picked up speed, Queenie's ears would fly back just a little. Sometimes she'd look back at me and actually smile. I'm sure of it! She showed all of her teeth and wagged her tail. To the amazement of my family, we never did fall.

Queenie would look a little worried, though, when I'd park the bike and put down the kickstand. The basket, now heavy with a small dog, would fall slightly to the left or right over the front tire. Even though I was always there to lift Queenie down, she'd have squeezed her eyebrows together into a worried frown, as if to say, *Hey! You aren't going to let me fall, are you?*

After our trips to the grocery store, we'd play dolls. You can guess who got to be the doll. I dressed Queenie up in doll clothes a neighbor lady had made for my doll (named Jane) that actually "drank" the contents of a little bottle and then wet her pants. She was about the same size as Queenie, but it was so much more fun to play with the dog. I'm sure Queenie loved it, too, because she never complained or tried to get out of the clothes, although she did stumble on occasion. When the dresses were too long, I'd fashion a ribbon belt around her chubby little waist to hold the fabric up off the floor. She seemed to think that was okay. With a quick polish of her toenails (all of them), we'd be off for a parade around the block, to the delight of our neighbors.

Putting baby bonnets on Queenie proved a little more difficult. Not that she would complain, try to turn her head away, or—heaven forbid—snap at me. But the bonnets were always too big for her small head, so we would have to improvise. Once I had the bonnet secured under her chin, though, all was right with the world—at least for me. As for Queenie, she looked pretty silly. But she didn't seem to care, so long as we were playing together.

Sometimes, after dressing Queenie in the doll clothes, I'd sit in our rocker in the living room, wrap her in a small blanket, and rock her like I might a baby, with all four of her feet sticking up out of the blanket. She never could keep those paws tucked into the blanket. I suppose I was just practicing to be a mom, and, again, Queenie didn't seem to mind. (It's pretty easy to see that I was an only child for a long, long time.)

My mother had to put my precious dog to sleep one day when I was at school, when I was twelve. I came home from school expecting to play with Queenie, as always, and Mother told me that she had died of a heart attack. Gone. Just like that. In the blink of an eye, my best friend in the whole world was gone. It would be many years before I would learn that Queenie had been diagnosed with an advanced stage of cancer, and my parents had decided the kindest thing to do was to have her put to sleep. But to this day, I question why they didn't offer me a chance to tell her how much I loved her and to give her one last kiss. They tried to save me the pain of having to tell her goodbye—just one of those decisions you make for your children, hoping you're doing the right thing. I'm sure it had pained them even more to see how deeply I grieved for Queenie.

For me now, even at my age, I still have a black and white photo of Queenie displayed on my refrigerator, and I still think of her every single day. She was the only friend I've ever had who was totally supportive and nonjudgmental. I've had other pets through the years and have loved and cared for them well, but Queenie still remains the queen of my heart.

I've often wondered if I meet Queenie in heaven one day, if she'll still have her toenails polished or if she'll be wearing one of my doll dresses with a baby bonnet tied under her chin. I wonder if she misses riding my bicycle with me, or if she knows how much I wish I could have told her goodbye.

I want to tell Queenie so many things, even to this day, but mostly I want her to know that it was never any fun for me to ride my bicycle after she was gone. I propped it up against the garage wall and rarely rode it again. I gave up playing dolls, too. There are just some things that can never be the same again without your best friend!

RUTH ANDREW is a writer living in Spokane, Washington. Previous short stories and humor articles have been published in newspapers and lifestyle magazines, including *My Mom Is My Hero*. Read about her at *www .iecrwa.com/bios/ruthandrew.html*.

Our Unexpected Hero, Schnauzer

JOYCE ROBINSON

Schnauzer was a purebred without clipped ears, so his gently fell around his gray, black and white face. Waving his tail high in the air, he would race as fast as the wind down the meadow, rich with tall green grasses and flowering white daisies. As he bounded up and down in the tall grasses, he would stretch his neck to see over them. Sometimes, he would come back home from his wanderings with a coat full of burs that we would gently pull from his back and around his nose.

Schnauzer was an inquisitive dog by nature, and one day he had been a little too inquisitive with a porcupine, with painful results. He came home with quills surrounding his face. What a pitiful face it was, and so sad. That was a painful reminder not to get too close to this new and strange creature with spikes and to give it a wide berth should he ever come into contact with it again.

And then there was the encounter with a skunk . . . we knew it before he came into view. The odor was so offensive, that we avoided him at all costs. It was quite a challenge avoiding his friendly licks and rubs. We tried shampooing him, but with no success. *Oh, don't you love me today?* his eyes would ask, as he tried desperately to rub up against us. He just didn't understand that we had to impatiently wait for the foul smell to wear off.

Schnauzer would let us know he was on duty by the loud howl he resounded as he chased stray brown rabbits across the field. Most times, the rabbit would reach its hole just in the nick of time. I can think of only one baby rabbit that lost the race, and when it did, Schnauzer reached down and picked up the baby bunny by its furry neck and gently carried it to us. He placed it on the ground in front of our feet, only to have it race off in the opposite direction as fast as its little feet could carry it. After he watched his prize catch run away, Schnauzer tilted his head to the side, his eyes full of confusion, and seemingly said, *I did my job, didn't I?* His big bright, brown eyes would always melt our hearts.

Whenever we ventured into the woods and the wide, wavy fields, Schnauzer trotted right beside us, acting very much like "just one of the kids." He loved to supervise our adventures and participate in every romp. If we tried to hide, he would shortly find us. That fuzzy face would nuzzle up from under someone's arm and reward us with a big, juicy lick on the face. He would then race around checking out the area with his nose, sniffing under every thin blade of grass or stray fallen leaf.

A family consisting of a mom, a dad, twin teenage girls, a younger sister, and little baby boy lived just down the road from us. Since we were all good friends, we played together often, and of course Schnauzer loved everyone, especially the children.

One bright sunny day, as Schnauzer was roaming his realm, he saw their toddler waddling down the gravel driveway. At that moment, our friendly neighborhood mailman was making his usual rounds. He had stopped at this family's mailbox, at the end of the long driveway. Just as the mailman leaned over to place the mail in the box, the toddler darted down the road and hid in front of the mailman's car, as if playing hide-and-seek. The mailman never saw him.

Schnauzer sensed that something was wrong and quickly ran along the side of the car. Then he moved to the front of the mailman's car, where he barked frantically and paced back and forth. The mailman had no idea that the toddler was standing in front of his car, but Schnauzer knew and stood his ground, refusing to move.

The mailman began shouting and waving his hands to shoo Schnauzer away, but our sweet dog refused to budge. Finally, the mailman got out of his car, hoping to chase the pesky dog away. Schnauzer eagerly beckoned the mailman to follow him. The mailman peered in the front, emitted a huge sigh of relief that he had not struck the toddler, and reached down and gently picked up the child. Clearly relieved—and thrilled—Schnauzer stopped barking and wagged his tail. He had saved his friend just in the nick of time. When the toddler's mother ran down the driveway and gratefully retrieved her young child, the mailman reached down and gave a big, loving pat to Schnauzer's head. Warm hugs from the grateful mom followed. Everyone praised my fuzzy, warm-hearted dog. Schnauzer was a real hero!

I would have never thought that my playful dog would sense the danger in that situation and immediately spring into action. Yet on this day, he became that small child's guardian angel. We never know who can be depended upon to take action. We were all so very surprised and proud to learn that our beloved Schnauzer had saved this young boy's life.

JOYCE ROBINSON is a semiretired grandmother who works in sales and advertising for Marks Products, Inc. She loved and grew up with an assortment of pets and farm animals, and she enjoys sharing their unique stories.

Five New Sets of Eyes

JANE ANGELICH

Belva, eight weeks without your fifty-five pounds of butt-wagging exuberance seems like a big price to pay, but seeing you with your five newest puppies makes me once again realize that your contribution to the blind is well worth the price.

You didn't know I was there, watching you on closed-circuit television with your two-day-old tiny balls of fur. You couldn't hear me proudly telling each passer-by that you are my Guide Dog breeder and these are your twelfth through sixteenth contributions to the eighteen-month journey that could ultimately provide a blind person with the independence that a cane could never give him or her. You didn't see the ear-to-ear smile on my face when you bent over to clean each of your new children and make sure they were okay.

Three classes of first-graders came to visit you and watched the monitor with me as you fed your babies. I'm not sure they really understood what you were doing in that blue wading pool with all the torn-up newspaper, but I tried to explain to them that you liked making those paper nests and cuddling with your three little girls and two little boys. They giggled as one of your boys climbed under your tail and took a nap. I had a long discussion with one first-grader who begged me to talk to her parents because she *really* needed a dog, and she wanted to buy all five. She wasn't happy with you or me or her parents that your puppies weren't going home with her!

Every day, I look at your pictures on my cell phone. I often show friends and strangers your goofy, missing-a-couple-of-teeth grin as I explain your "job" and the important work that you do. I study the pictures of your little body as it grew over your eight-plus weeks of pregnancy and am still amazed how all those puppies fit into that small space. I check the sonogram pictures and think about the day you went for your exam. You stayed still for the ten minutes that the doctor had you on your back like you were enjoying a "spa day." How come you never stay still that long when I'm trying to brush you?

By the last week of your pregnancy, you were eating six times your usual helpings, and your satisfied belches assured me that you enjoyed every last bite of it. You are going to have to readjust to smaller quantities when you return home to get back your girlish figure, young lady.

Also, your dad and I were going to let this one go, but I think you can handle this one teensy complaint. We have been finding a few holes in the backyard, and we know you put them there. Can't blame it on the deer, since the yard is totally fenced in. We have forgiven you because we know you were preparing birthing areas, just in case we didn't get you to the delivery room on time, and we felt you should have known us by now and realized that we do much better with your medical needs than we do with our own.

By the way, your son, Rafferty, from your second litter, graduated from the Guide Dog Program. You were "too pregnant," so I attended the graduation ceremony without you. It was a beautiful, sunny day on campus, and I sat under a tree watching Rafferty as he majestically marched onstage and was ceremonially given to a lovely wife and mother from Canada. The man who raised and trained Rafferty told stories of your son's well-behaved and brilliant beginnings. By the way, he looks like you—black and shiny, but just a little bit bigger. Luckily, I took plenty of tissues with me and used every one of them as I cried through the entire ceremony.

You missed my conversation with Rafferty's new owner and the tears in her eyes as she told me of the leap of faith it required to surrender her cane after three decades and to put all of her trust in your son. I assured her that your boy was going to take excellent care of her and that she could look forward to years of outings with her family and friends. Without question, Rafferty was going to be her hero.

And as I wait for you to come home, dear Belva, there is one more thing you don't know. Yesterday, your dad and I learned that we are going to be grandparents. For years, we have been telling people we are grandparents to all of your puppies, but now we know how it feels to anticipate our first nonfurry grandchild. And wow, are we excited!

So, hurry home, Belva. We have a lot of planning to do for the next birth. After all, you're the one with sixteen successful children under your belt, and I've still got a lot to learn.

JANE ANGELICH is the mother of two sons, ages thirty-two and twenty-five, and a newly minted mother-in-law. Her second book, *What's a Mother (In-Law) to Do? The 5 Essential Steps to Building a Loving Relationship with Your Son's Wife*, was released by Simon & Schuster in 2009. She lives with her husband, a firefighter, and their two Guide Dogs for the Blind Labrador retrievers in Marin County, California.

The Widget Dance

KAREN BAKER

I had wanted a dog with a big bark, one to protect my daughter against danger, like Lassie, a dog I had watched on television as a child. After all, we lived in the country adjacent to a forest of pines, madrones, and black oaks, a thickly treed home for mountain lions and rattlesnakes. My daughter, Mercedes, however, chose a fox terrier puppy, one so small that she could cup its wriggling body in both hands. She named her Widget, and that black and white pup grew into a spunky dog—but oddly enough, one that never barked.

Most dogs bark in play, but not Widget. Even when she and Mercedes chased each other or played hide and seek among the trees, Widget rarely made a sound. She grew into a companion, not a protector; they became inseparable, Mercedes with her ponytail swinging and Widget bounding alongside her, eyes alert, ears perked, and her tail a blur. That terrier even curled up amid the dolls when Mercedes and her schoolgirl friends gathered to play, tilting her patient head to one side as Barbie dolls in fancy dresses "walked over her" on their way to gala parties or proms. Never a whimper. Never a complaint.

In the mornings, after Mercedes stepped onto the school bus, that little dog stood on her pencil legs and watched until the bus rumbled out of sight; then she became my dog, my little helper. She trotted beside me through the pasture to feed our one-ton bulls and thousand-pound cows. Although small, she stood guard at the open barn door. With throaty growls and the snap of her teeth, she turned back cattle trying to break into the stack of hay. Inside our house, she "helped" me clean the kitchen, ferreting out every crumb or tidbit that had fallen under the table during breakfast. Her nails clicked along behind me, following me from room to room as I washed laundry, vacuumed, or mopped. In the vegetable garden, she dug for moles when I weeded, but at 4:00 P.M. she started the "Widget dance," her terrier pirouette, leaping high into the air, twirling around and landing on her paws, then staring me down with those round, brown eyes. She repeated the dance until I responded, "Okay, Widget. Okay. It must be time to pick up Mercedes," and off we'd walk down our dusty road to the bus.

On weekends, the three of us often picnicked under the grape arbor, my daughter and I with our sandwiches, Widget with her doggie treats. When Mercedes became a young teen, she stepped away from me and became secretive as she talked to new friends about dances, high school gossip, and boys. During this time, Widget, with her constant wags and pink-tongue kisses, gave my adolescent a type of love I couldn't give. That little dog never had to greet her with the mad-mother face about chores left undone. She never questioned her about her comings and goings or the completion of her homework. She never embarrassed her by phoning other parents and insisting on adult supervision for Friday-night functions, those that "everyone else" could attend. Unlike me, Widget never had to say "no" and never brought tears to Mercedes' eyes. Sometimes, I'd look down at Widget and say, "It's going to take the two of us to get this girl raised." Looking up at me, she'd cock her head and wag her tail as if she understood.

One afternoon, I watched Mercedes from the living room as she headed to the patio, out of earshot, with the phone snuggled to her ear, chatting and laughing with a friend. As she meandered in slow circles over the pebbled cement, Widget cut in front of her, darting back and forth, nudging at her feet and legs. Mercedes kept talking until she finally reached down, stroked the little dog and said, "Later. We'll play later."

Widget turned and raced toward the living room, where I was sitting, and hurtled herself against the sliding glass door, the pads of all four paws banging against it. She continued springing up and down, at least three feet in the air, hitting and rehitting the slider. Thinking it was a new "Let me in" Widget dance, I opened the door—but instead of coming in, she sped across the lawn back to the patio.

Nothing seemed wrong; still I called out to Mercedes, "Everything okay?"

She answered with an audible sigh, "Fine, Mom."

I closed the door, but in a flash that streak of black and white reappeared. This time our quiet dog barked. A wild, attention-getting bark. An urgent "there-isn't-a-minute-to-waste" bark.

Those worried eyes, that wrinkled brow, and that insistent bark demanded that I follow. She ran to Mercedes, then past her, lunging toward the kitchen door, bristled and stiff-legged, tense from the tip of her tail to the tip of her nose. At first, I saw nothing. Then I spotted it under the lip of our doorway, a deadly diamond-backed danger blended into the shadow. Fanged and venomous, a rattlesnake hid within striking distance of Mercedes. Somehow, Widget had spotted it or smelled it or sensed it, so close to the one she loved. She stood between Mercedes and the rattlesnake until the snake slithered back into the wild, leaving Mercedes safe. Widget's devoted eyes, ears, nose, and that special sense were priceless. I wished I could have sent Widget to watch over Mercedes as she stepped out into the world.

That little terrier's actions rivaled all the miracle saves I had seen on television as a child, ones that I knew were just pretend but in my heart wanted to believe. Widget protected, just like Lassie. When she couldn't, she ran for help, just like Lassie. She was not a big dog with a big bark, but just as big of a heroine, a real heroine, our little Widget.

KAREN BAKER lives in northern California with two dogs, eight cats, two horses, several sheep, and a herd of cattle, many of whom helped in her "mothering duties" for her three daughters. She works with her husband, a practicing veterinarian. Karen has won awards in writing contests and is published in the Jessamyn West literary anthology of contest winners.

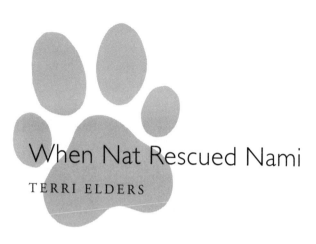

When Nat Rescued Nami

TERRI ELDERS

"It's hard to be brave when you're only a Very Small Animal."
—Piglet

Tsunami, also known as Nami, our two-year-old purebred Akita, did not take readily to our new country home. When my husband, Ken, and I lived in Silver Spring, Maryland, we took Nami to the dog park for a romp at least twice a week. She played beach ball soccer with the other dogs and permitted curious toddlers to unfurl her trademark tail. She even stood patiently while adults oohed and aahed over her white foreleg markings, so symmetrical that one lady actually called across the field to ask where I had purchased her cute snow boots.

However, now we lived in retirement far from such civilized canine playgrounds. Because our pastures were fenced with barbed wire, easy for even a large dog to crawl under, Nami could play outside only on her nylon lead. We had hooked two together for a 40-foot range and provided her with an array of Kongs, balls, and rope toys. But when we put her out to romp, Nami would just give her Kong a listless nudge or the ball a disconsolate sideways kick, and then she'd plop down and yawn.

Our veterinarian neighbor's trio of retired racehorses roamed on the other side of the fence. Whenever they emitted a snort, nicker, or whinny, Nami would glance disdainfully in their direction, making it clear that she knew they were some other strange species, not tall dogs, and certainly not worthy of much interest.

We learned that people frequently left litters at The Flour Mill, a local feed store, in hopes that the unwanted kittens, pups, or bunnies would be adopted. I brought home three little kittens, but Ken warned me that Nami probably would regard them as potential snacks rather than playmates. Other than offering an occasional halfhearted growl of annoyance though, Nami simply appeared bored with the kittens' antics.

"We have to get her a pet," Ken announced after another week had gone by. He headed for the Mill that afternoon and came back with a seven-week-old livewire, a shaggy black mongrel with a dapper white chest. "A notice on the litter box said that his dad was a Great Pyrenees and his mom a Heinz 57 combo," he said, handing me the wiggling ball of fur.

The pup didn't weigh much more than the kittens. "He looks so natty," I said. "I'm calling him Natty." "I'm calling him Nat then," Ken rejoined. "No diminutives for my buddy here."

We took Nat out to the yard where Nami was dozing in the sun. He bounded over, climbed up her flank, and nibbled on her ear. For the first time since we moved, Nami perked up. All day she lay in patient contentment while the puppy gnawed her ankle, swatted her nose with his tiny paw, and curled up under her chin to sleep.

They remained inseparable, Nat trotting after Nami as she roamed the yard. He began to join her in batting the balls, in playing tug-of-war with the fringed ropes, and in chasing the kittens if they strayed into their territory. He soon learned that he could play keep-away tag with Nami, running just outside the circumference of her lead. As Nat grew, they began to wrestle, and Nami sometimes rolled over and let him win. Apparently, she knew how to keep her playmate motivated to continue the contests.

Then one winter afternoon while the dogs gamboled in the yard, I ducked into the house for a moment. When I returned, they were gone. Nami's hooked-together nylon leads had somehow come unsnapped.

Ken and I drove up and down the nearby roads, stopping now and then to call their names. Alas, they had vanished, most likely into the surrounding hills. "Don't worry," Ken reassured me. "When they get tired of roaming, they'll come home." But I did worry. Nami was trailing that nylon lead behind her, and I kept imagining it getting tangled in shrubbery, trapping her in the woods.

A little after sundown, while Ken drove off again to search, I went outside to call their names. After a few minutes, I thought I heard sounds from the back pasture. Sure enough, here came Nat, panting, damp, and out of breath. He flopped down at my feet, tongue hanging out and eyes wild. I bent and patted him. "Where's Nami . . . where's your Nami?" I pleaded.

Nat kept staring back across the pasture from whence he came. I began to shiver in the icy, moonless night. "Natty, where's Nami?" I asked once more. Nat, still panting, lurched to his feet and trotted back across the dark field. I thought I heard some distant growls and grunts. Soon I could make out Nat's white patch on his small, dark form as he slowly trudged toward me. Then I saw the much larger Nami limping behind. As they drew closer, I saw that Nat had Nami's nylon lead in his mouth. After every step or two, the pair paused. Then Nat took a few short steps more and tugged on the lead, and Nami inched forward. It took a while, but they finally made it to the house, Nami moving more and more haltingly. She barely made it up the step to the side door, and then she heaved herself inside and collapsed on the carpet.

"They came home, but she's hurt," I told Ken when he returned. "There's something wrong with her legs, but Nat brought her out of the pasture with her lead in his mouth." Ken gave me a skeptical glance. "Are you sure? That sounds highly improbable."

"I saw it, Ken. Natty brought her home from the field."

The next morning we took Nami to the vet. She had ruptured her anterior cruciate ligaments and would need surgery. Apparently she had been jumping over fences on their excursion, and large dogs such as Akitas are prone to such injuries, the vet explained. Nami underwent two operations, one leg at a time, and Natty remained by her side during the weeks of her recovery.

Once on her feet, we had the backyard securely chain-linked so the pair could play outdoors freely.

Nami's nearing six now, and Nat's four. Though Nami will always be the larger, they still wrestle as equals, still play tug-of-war, and remain inseparable. Nami remains the alpha dog, a regal queen reigning over her backyard realm. Natty, her devoted servant, more loyal than royal, still grabs and gulps and follows her faithfully.

He may never merit a crown, but as our brave hero, he certainly earned his medal. His new dog tag reads: "Natty, Rescuer."

TERRI ELDERS won UCLA's Community Service Award in 2006 for her work overseas with the Peace Corps and domestically with VISTA. She and her husband, Ken Wilson, live in the country outside Colville, Washington, with two dogs and three cats. Her stories of family, friends and furred companions have appeared in *Chicken Soup for the Soul, Cup of Comfort®,* and other anthologies, including *My Dad Is My Hero.*

The Labrador Way

LESE DUNTON

They told me I could have the pick of the litter. "Great," I said. "What does that mean?"

It meant that my parents had allowed our Labrador retriever to have his way with their friend's female Lab. Both dogs had pedigrees and were beautifully black. The reward? A five-year-old, that's me, got to choose any puppy she wanted from the arranged canine marriage. The cutest offspring would belong to me and no one else. Mine, all mine—a little girl's dream.

I remember being surrounded by soft, cuddly puppies jumping for my attention. As their bodies stumbled and maneuvered playfully, their big, brown eyes stayed steady and calm. This was the most difficult and fun decision I had made in all of my five years.

Just as the choice seemed impossible, a little guy from the back caught my eye. He was shimmering with joy. He had an air of a confidence about him, as if he'd eaten a canary and was laughing inside. He knew he was destined to be mine. It was merely a matter of getting his brothers and sisters out of the way.

He headed right toward me, wiggling to the left and to the right with great force, bumping aside his siblings one by one. When he reached the front of the pack, he looked up at me again, in love. I pointed my finger straight at him to signal the adults. And when a little girl says, "That one," she means it.

My parents lifted him into their arms high above me. I was horrified when they used a big pair of scissors to snip off a chunk of his hair. Mom reassured me this was simply a way to separate him from the others; it wouldn't hurt, and his hair would grow back.

I didn't feel entirely comfortable again until the puppy lay in my lap sleeping as we sat in the back seat of our Oldsmobile Vista Cruiser station wagon heading home. His little whiskers were itching my leg, but I didn't dare move; his well-being became my life's purpose from that moment on.

We named him Paddles because all Labradors like to paddle in the water, any water. My first choice was to call him Blacky, for obvious reasons: He was black and children have a tendency to add the letter "y" to things they like. My parents said "no," for unspoken reasons, but the name Paddles was cool, so I went with it.

By the following day, it became clear that this four-legged angel, who appeared in my world so sweetly, had talents that were best revealed in a dog show. Convinced he would win first place, I announced this plan to my mother, and she agreed. When I was older, she made a confession: "The only reason we let you do it was because we wanted to show you that it's not that simple. You can't just think up things and do them and always expect they'll work out." I'm grateful she held off on telling me this.

I remember training Paddles every day. The book said not to go more than five to ten minutes because puppies don't have a long attention span. Day after day, Paddles and I worked on his ability to sit perfectly motionless, head up, paws just so, looking straight ahead. Then we practiced walking back and forth briskly without a leash, close to my leg but not touching. Paddles was good. Really good.

My mother had to attend official and mysterious dog show meetings that did not allow little girls, sadly. She did bring me back a Rockland County Kennel Club pen, which I held tightly in my little hands. It became one of my most cherished possessions.

By the time of the big show, I was a six-year-old, love-filled dog trainer, and my one-year-old Paddles was a master of his craft. Highly intuitive, he knew what you wanted. His moves were impeccably graceful and solid. His kind face was sleek, as though a sculptor had carefully made it smooth. I loved kissing him on the forehead, but not with so many people around.

"Look at the little girl! Look at the little girl!" I kept hearing people say. I guess compared with our final competitor, a gray-haired man, I must have looked very young indeed.

Perhaps competing against a child created too much pressure for the opposing team. When it came time for the walking-briskly-back-and-forth-close-to-the-knee routine (the hardest one), the gray-haired man's dog jumped up and down nervously. Major demerits.

Paddles and I, on the other hand, appeared the picture of calm. No doubts or fears. I couldn't believe how elegantly he executed all procedures. His body trotted alongside me at just the right distance and pace; head held evenly, and then stopping in unison, paw to foot. Amazing.

When they handed us the trophy, it sparkled in the sun. The ribbon said, "Best of Show, Puppy Division."

As we pulled in the driveway, my mother honked the horn over and over, sounding a victory to my father and older brothers waiting at home. No one thought to have a camera ready, because no one thought we would win—except Paddles and me. It didn't matter. I have the picture in my mind forever.

After that, we both relaxed. The necessary limitations of dog show rules gave way to unrestrained excitement and open-air playfulness. I tried to run after Paddles, but he was too fast. He'd leap into the air to catch a tennis ball or jump in the water to make a big splash, and then paddle gracefully back to shore so he could do it all over again. And on some sad days ahead, he would look at me with quiet compassion when I cried.

The moral to the story is to go after what your heart imagines would be fun, and don't listen to the doubts of sensible grown-ups. A dog can teach you that.

Paddles passed on when I was eighteen. When he shows up in my dreams now, he is always wiggling with joy.

LESE DUNTON is the founder, editor, and even publisher of the *New Sun* (www.newsun.com). She enjoys the beauty of nature in all seasons and the variety of surprises in her hometown, New York.

The Bond

KATHRYN GODSIFF

Through all the training and love lavished on Sheena in her active life, she remained . . . a dog. The soulful wisdom of the ages wasn't reflected in her big, brown eyes; she was begging for a treat. She didn't understand telepathically that I wanted her to stop, sit, and stay; she watched my body for subtle clues, knowing there would be a reward for getting it right.

Those doggy traits kept me grounded through the years that Sheena walked and worked with me. I was a practical farmer working with my husband and raising three sons on a sheep and cattle farm in New Zealand. I understood that dogs weren't furry people. Our working dogs were appreciated for their role on the farm. No matter what we did or said, those dogs leapt up enthusiastically every morning, lived outside, and cheerfully ate old, tough sheep my husband regularly butchered for their dinner.

Still, I entertained thoughts of a faithful family dog, one that would recognize us in a crowd and come running. I wanted our boys to have sweet memories of a special pet. And I hankered after a dog for me, to tramp the hills with, one who'd nestle close as the sun went down. I got all that in Sheena, bless her golden heart. I also got a dog that loved to roll in dead things, eat calf poop, and chase possums.

Sheena, a slightly timid golden retriever, was born on 8/8/88, one of eight puppies in the litter. She was the only dog her breeder ever had returned to her, due to the divorce of Sheena's owners when she was ten months old. At the time, I was looking for an older, housetrained puppy. The day we met, Sheena wriggled a bit like pups do, and then she sat quietly while my fingers explored the softness of her smooth, butter-colored coat. I just knew we'd forge a world-class bond.

Her basic obedience was just enough to keep her in sight, unless a rabbit bounced out from a bush. Then she'd give chase, never catching up but having a great run. She embraced the river behind our house like retrievers do and ran before my horse as I rode across the hills on our farm.

During Sheena's second year, I heard of a search-dog training group in our area, and we joined. Dogs and handlers were being prepared to take part in searches for lost people. Over the next three years, Sheena became a talented and successful search dog. I learned how to be an effective trainer, and she learned to resist the smells that tempt dogs everywhere. Her focus was on a human scent while we were searching. The gleeful and uncontrolled dashes into the bushes became a thing of the past, mostly. We were on the road to The Bond.

There were a few bumpy patches along the way. One moonless night my husband had to be away from the farm. Sheena normally slept in our laundry room, but this night, because I was a bit nervous about being alone, she would sleep beside the half-empty bed.

At bedtime, Sheena went out to do her business. When I called her, I was met with silence. I called louder and louder, finally yelling at the top of my lungs (you can do that when your nearest neighbor is a half-mile away). Still no Sheena. Slamming my feet into Wellies and yanking a jacket over my flannel nightie, I stomped out into the night, waving a flashlight around and shouting some more. Finally I heard the faint jingle of her tags, and then I smelled an odor most foul. Sheena came panting up to me, wagging her tail and sporting a big patch of greenish ooze on her back from the dead sheep she'd found at the top of the hill. I didn't know whether to laugh, cry, or scream. What I did do was take a deep breath and drag Sheena into the bathroom for a midnight bath. I was devastated—how could she have done this doggy thing on a night when I needed her devotion and protection?

I brought out the worst punishment I could think of: the blow dryer. She looked crestfallen at the consequences of her night of splendor; I felt crushed that The Bond was so tenuous. She should have known that I was a bit frightened to be alone and needed her by my side.

In the light of day, waking up to a sweet-smelling dog next to the bed, I realized that The Bond I wanted was a romantic creation. Sure, Sheena respected my place as the alpha female, and she preferred my company to that of any other human. But she was still a dog, living on a farm and doing farm-dog things. This revelation opened my heart to a whole new aspect of The Bond.

When Sheena and I were working on a search, and she flushed a possum or rabbit, it was my responsibility to act quickly to arrest her flight. If I missed the moment, I had a lot of hiking to do to get her back. When I noticed her sniffing around on our walks on the farm, if I didn't call her back and she found something to roll in or eat, tough luck for my nose.

I don't think dogs knowingly test The Bond. Once it's there, it's there. It's the humans who have the need to make sure it's still intact.

Sheena and I got a somewhat public assessment of our connection out on the farm one day. Four of us were moving several hundred sheep and needed to get them through a tricky gateway. We had some electric-fence tape in the truck and tied one end to the gatepost, creating a laneway down the length of the tape (which wasn't electrified, by the way). It was a few meters short of the next place to tie it off, and while my husband, one of our sons, and the hired hand scratched their heads, I tied the end to Sheena's collar and told her to stay. It was a gamble; Sheena was still timid around the animals, and if she ran off we'd be in a big mess with the sheep. We disappeared to do the gather, with me hoping for the best and the men looking skeptical.

The ewes streamed down the hills toward the gate, a mass of white against the brown of late-summer grass. They raced past the furry, golden "post" toward the tricky gate and into the next pasture. Sheena sat still as a stone throughout the whole operation. When I untied her, she was trembling but ready for her reward—a fast game of tug-of-war. I was cool in the face of my companions' amazement, but inside I was turning cartwheels. Who cared if Sheena rolled in gunk and brought home cow bones to chew? We did indeed have The Bond.

KATHRYN GODSIFF lives in Sisters, Oregon, these days, managing a small ranch with her husband and bonding with her Boston terrier. She is a freelance writer whose work has been published in *My Mom Is My Hero*, *A Cup of Comfort® for Dog Lovers*, and *Chick Ink: 40 Stories of Women and Their Tattoos*.

Red Dog

LOGAN BRANJORD

As a youth in the Wisconsin countryside, I had all the back-yard, woods, fields, lakes, and rivers a boy could want. While perfect for any outdoor activity, it presented one major problem: no friends. For me to find a playmate, I had to trek at least five miles on my bike. Moreover, I spent the majority of my time doing chores for my parents, which left little time to make that bike ride and see my pals.

My parents' solution to my problem was Red Dog, a giant, lumbering golden retriever who became the best companion I could have had. Red Dog had a thick torso and tail and an ever-lasting, almost comical, smile. His coat grew in so thick, brushing it became nearly impossible. We had to do it once in a great while, but we felt so bad for him we wouldn't do it again for another month. Luckily, Red Dog wasn't picky.

I'd wake up hours before my parents every day, for one reason or another, and the boredom of having to remain quiet while waiting for them to rise nearly drove me mad. I solved the problem by taking sojourns into the fields, looking for snakes or lizards. Red Dog never missed a walk. The second I opened the door he would rush to my side, and off we would go for hours. I liked having Red Dog by my side, and he apparently felt similarly as he would never wander too far from me. With Red Dog I knew we would always rustle up a hiding rabbit or grouse from the briar, which certainly added excitement to our hikes. When Red Dog looked tired, and the dew on the leaves and grass started to dry up, I knew it was time to go home.

During the evening, Red ate only the finest meals. We always gave him his own breast of chicken or a small slab of juicy marbled meat, but this was never enough. Once, when my father went inside to grab a plate and inadvertently left the top of the grill open, Red Dog poked his head around the corner of the house and stole whole pieces of chicken one at a time. They were so hot he would pull them off the grill (burning some of his fur in the process) and drop them on the ground immediately to keep from burning his mouth. We caught him red-pawed, but he looked so hilarious we couldn't stay mad, especially when he realized he was busted, grabbed his chicken, and ran away to eat it in peace. You had to love him.

Red Dog was also sociable. The neighbors across the river had a wild cocker spaniel named Sparks. Once in awhile, that unruly dog would swim across the river and play with Red Dog. In the winter, the Apple River would ice over partially but not enough for Sparks to cross, even though he often tested his luck. Typically, Sparks would turn back when he reached the edge of the ice, but we all knew it was a matter of time before he would fall in. Red, on the other hand, never set one paw on that ice.

One day Sparks stepped out too close to the edge of the ice and, when it gave way, fell into the icy water. Sparks let loose a piercing yelp and tried to paddle back onto the ice, but his paws couldn't catch hold. As he madly dog-paddled to keep his nose above water, my dad and I readied the canoe for a rescue mission. To our astonishment, however, Red Dog had already taken to the ice himself and was racing to rescue Sparks.

Terrified that Red Dog would drown, we shouted, "Oh, no! Reeeddd! Here, Red Dog!" But he was paddling madly toward Sparks, who was already beginning to give up swimming, and didn't heed our calls.

By the time my dad slid the canoe out to the edge of the ice, poor Sparks had disappeared under the surface, and Red was struggling as well. As soon as he reached him, my dad grabbed Red Dog by the collar and pulled him by his midsection up to the edge of the ice. I was worried the canoe might tip while he tried—with or without a life vest, it was easy to die in freezing river water. Fortunately, Red Dog lodged his front and hind legs on the lip of the ice and pulled himself to safety. Sparks remained just out of reach, so my dad slid the wooden paddle under his belly and pulled him toward the ice. Poor Sparks was so exhausted, my dad had to drag him up onto the ice by his jingling collar.

My mother and I hopped into the car and sped six miles, crossing the bridge upstream to pick Red Dog up from the opposite side of the river. Once he was safely in the car, wrapped in a blanket, shivering but obviously very much alive, none of us could quite believe that our cautious and wise Red Dog had so willingly endangered his own life to rescue Sparks. Just imagine what he'd be willing to do for us!

LOGAN BRANJORD is a hardworking writer living in the icy retreats of northern Wisconsin. He spends his time outdoors sledding and shoveling or indoors reading by the fireplace. If you spot an error, you can blame his wild kitten, "Bear," for scampering across the keyboard during the process.

Dual Heroines

DAVID L. AUGUSTYN

S ara Eldridge Tag Along, an orange and white purebred Brittany spaniel, and Gloria, my wife, forged a bond that allowed one mother to trust the other with the lives of her offspring.

It all started during Tag's pregnancy, when she developed pneumonia and Gloria nursed her back to health. A few weeks after her recovery, I got the call that the pups were coming. When the kids and I arrived home, we were astonished to see Gloria down on the floor helping Tag deliver her pups.

Tag, the worrywart, stood for each pup she delivered while Gloria encouraged her. Gloria would "catch" each pup, cut the umbilical cord and place the pup in front of Tag so she could remove the birth sac and finish by licking the pup clean. Then Tag would arrange them in the "birthing box."

That day Tag, with Gloria's help, delivered nine healthy pups. That was unusual for a Brittany, as they normally have litters of only four or five. But the delivery was not over yet. One more was struggling to be born. Tag was having difficulty and was getting stressed, as this one was not coming easily. This struggle went on for what seemed like an hour. Yet Gloria would not leave Tag. Finally, ever so slowly, the birth sac emerged. You could see the relief on Tag's and Gloria's faces. But something was wrong. Tag was not able to lick the sac off. Gloria picked it up and laid it on the table. Tag anxiously watched as Gloria cut the unusually thick sac off the pup. Tag immediately started to lick the pup, but it seemed lifeless. She looked worriedly at Gloria. Gloria quickly placed her mouth over the pup's nostrils and mouth and breathed gently. She followed that by pushing lightly on its chest with her fingers. She opened the pup's mouth to check for blockage and repeated breathing gently into his nostrils and pushing lightly on his chest over and over again. After what seemed a long time, the pup yelped and began to move and breathe. Tag jumped in circles excitedly. Gloria placed the pup in front of the anxiously waiting mother. Tag finished the job of cleaning the pup. He was much bigger than the others, thus the difficulty in delivery. We could see the pup had an umbilical hernia as a result of the delivery.

The next morning, Gloria called the veterinarian and made arrangements for a checkup. Her brother carried the box with the pups while Gloria carried Tag, who had collapsed in the parking lot from fear of the vet. The office was abuzz with excitement to see ten new Brittany spaniels. Each pup was taken out of the box, weighed, checked over, and given a good bill of health except for number ten, whose hernia was confirmed. He would have to come back for an operation to correct the condition. While all this was going on, Tag had been placed on the table next to the pups so she could see that everything was all right. As the doctor checked each pup, Tag performed her own check. She was funny that way.

The doctor told Gloria that Tag would not be able to take care of ten pups and that she should be prepared in the event that Tag would either ignore two of the pups or that she might kill two of them. When asked what she could do about this, the vet suggested that Gloria try to bottle feed them every couple of hours but cautioned that it would probably not help. Also, in order for Tag to have milk rich enough to nourish that many pups, we were instructed to supplement her diet with two pounds of boiled hamburger per day. Tag did not mind this addition one little bit!

As predicted, Tag kept the two smallest pups between her front paws while the other eight suckled. Gloria prepared the puppy formula, placed it in the tiny bottles, and offered to feed one of the little pups. Tag immediately stood, shaking the "eight" loose from her teats, a very anxious, worried expression on her face. Gloria offered Tag the bottle; she drank it all, approved of it apparently, then sat down and watched as Gloria fed the smallest pup. From then on, when Tag fed the eight, Gloria fed the two smallest pups until they were large enough to compete with the others for their turn at Tag's teats.

We had to take all ten back to the vet's to have their tails docked and dew claws removed. Again Tag checked each pup over closely, giving her approval. We left the "big guy" there for the umbilical hernia repair, picking him up the next day. We couldn't tell if Tag missed him because, by this time, she was really busy. The "big guy" healed quickly, not missing a beat with the others.

The pups grew fast and had full reign of the kitchen for several weeks and then had to be moved into the backyard kennel. It was so nice to see them romping around as a family having fun and watch Tag break up fights between the pups. They were a very exciting attraction for the neighborhood kids.

Gloria watched over them as if they were her own kids. She fed them their bottles, boiled hamburger, and made sure they had all the puppy food they could eat. Now that they were eating solids, she also handled the "cleanup."

After all the pups were weaned, on full solid food, and had their shots, I put them up for sale. It was a difficult thing to do, but we could not keep ten pups. Over the next several weeks, one by one, they left the family. We hoped the new owners would take good care of them. It was so sad to see them leave, but it did teach the kids about life . . . and letting go. I did keep one pup for myself–the "big guy," DaCaSaGa, using our initials as a name for him. We called him Dac (Doc) for short. Doc and I became inseparable. He also became the best hunting dog I ever had. He had his mother's strength, determination, drive, intelligence, and love.

There were dual heroines throughout this experience: Tag for her strength, determination, and care, as well as Gloria, who endured with Tag to the point of saving a life.

DAVID L. AUGUSTYN had a true adventure article published in *Ontario Out of Doors* magazine as told to author Ted Gosline, and an essay titled "The Great Sower and Reaper" in the book *Field of Miracles,* edited by Jerry and Tine Wilkins. He is currently working on a collection of stories about the six dogs in his life.

Honor

NANCY BAKER

"Maribel, Maribel! This is the hospital. Do you need help?"

"Woof, woof!" replied Honor, Maribel's service dog.

"Maribel, what's going on?"

"Woof, woof!" was the response once again.

The light dawned on the confused hospital operator. "Maribel needs help. Honor is calling," she shouted to the nearby emergency medical technicians. And thus Honor became the legendary dog who called for an ambulance.

Maribel suffered from a nerve condition that robbed her legs of feeling. She was wheelchair-bound, and doctors had told her that she would no longer be able to live alone. They advised that she give up her home and reside in an assisted-living facility. As it turned out, she received assistance from a totally unexpected source: a five-year-old service dog named Honor.

Encouraged by friends, Maribel tackled the forty-page Texas Hearing and Service Dog (THSD) application, submitted it, and waited. When she had almost given up hope, THSD accepted her application, with a caveat: she would have a three-year wait, too long for her situation.

Maribel resigned herself to what she believed to be the inevitable, until a miracle occurred. THSD had matched her with Honor, a gentle, dark-red golden retriever who had been rescued from the streets. Sick with heartworms, Honor first had to be treated and then trained. So she waited a while longer, but when Maribel and Honor finally met, they experienced love at first sight. Honor quickly became invaluable to Maribel and delighted in helping her. She was trained to press handicapped buttons to open doors, stand firm to act as a brace, turn on lights, retrieve dropped articles, and to call for help.

While visiting Maribel, I learned the story. "*How* does a dog call for help?" I asked.

"I have a lifeline that connects directly to the hospital. Honor was trained to push a button on command to call them. Want to hear about the famed phone call?"

"Yes, I can hardly wait."

"Well, I was on my deck, enjoying a balmy spring day. I had a new swing and was lazily pushing it back and forth. Suddenly, without warning, it collapsed," Maribel explained.

"Oh, no!"

"Oh, yes," Maribel said, putting a hand to her head. "A 4 by 6 beam struck me on the head and a protruding bolt cut a gash—one that required thirty-one staples to close it. Alone, I would have bled to death, but I wasn't alone. Luckily, Honor was with me."

"What did she do?"

"Well," Maribel said, "I was unconscious, but Honor somehow moved the beam and then licked my face until I responded. I gave her the command to press the button."

"And, she did it?"

"You bet. I could hear the operator when she answered the phone." Maribel's eyes reflected amusement as she recalled the telephone operator trying to carry on a conversation with a dog.

Honor's fame spread. Paul Harvey related her story to the radio world, and it's still being shown on Animal Planet. Civic groups and schools often invited Honor to demonstrate her talents. On one such occasion, as Honor patiently posed with each of the children in the preschool class, Maribel noticed Honor had an unusual amount of drool and was unsteady. After the vet conducted an examination of Honor, he discovered a malignant brain tumor.

Maribel rebelled—*no, not Honor.* Not her precious friend, her brave hero, her faithful helper for only six short years. *No, this could not be.* But it was. Honor's decline was swift and unrelenting. Within weeks, Maribel had to face the unthinkable decision all dog lovers dread—when to put a pet to sleep.

On the tragic day, the veterinary technician escorted Maribel into a comfortable room and asked her to sit on a couch. She informed Maribel that they would bring Honor to her so she could rest her head on Maribel's lap as the fateful injection was administered. Heart heavy, Maribel covered her face and prepared as best she could for her last encounter with Honor.

"She doesn't look sick, does she?" the technician said, as he brought Honor to her master.

Maribel lifted her eyes to find Honor, true to her name and the courage she always displayed, walking toward her.

Shaking his head, the technician said, "She refused to let us carry her."

Honor stopped at Maribel's knee and raised her paw, as was her custom, in salutation. Gently, the technician placed Honor on the couch, where she snuggled against Maribel, placing her head in her lap. Maribel stroked her beloved dog's silky head and murmured to her, "Honor is such a good dog, such a good dog." Her voice broke as Honor suffered yet another seizure. Maribel sadly nodded her head, directing the technician to give the fateful injection.

Even though Honor had been gone for several years when I was being told this story, and Maribel has a wonderful new service dog, I noticed a tear slipping from Maribel's eye. "Oh, Maribel, how sad," I said.

"Perhaps Honor has gone to a place just this side of heaven," she mused, "where she has been restored to health and can run and play with other dogs waiting for their human companions. When the Lord calls me home, Honor will look up from her play and see me coming, and oh, our reunion will be ever so joyous. Then, we'll cross over together."

NANCY BAKER resides in College Station, Texas, with her husband and golden retriever, Alex, who once devoured an entire cheesecake and then grinned. She has been published in numerous anthologies and national magazines. Her favorite stories are about animal companions.

Goofy Willy

LINDA O'CONNELL

Willy, a naughty mischief-maker, annoyed half the residents in the wilderness town of Delta Junction, Alaska. The other 250 thought his antics were amusing. He was as thick in the head as he was in stature. Half hound dog and half Mackenzie River husky, he was definitely ruled by his comical hound dog genes. He roamed the woods near the end of the Alaska Highway; he snooped, swiped things, and sauntered around town like he owned it. His distinctive bark, "aahhrrooo," always preceded him up the gravel roads and through the tiny town. He was known by all. By the time he was six months old, it was apparent that Willy had inherited his short, brown coat from his mother and his stocky, seventy-pound build from his father. His eyelids and a handful of neck flab drooped, and he never outgrew his big-oaf, puppy clumsiness.

One cold fall morning, when the temperature rose slightly above freezing, Willy bounded out the door and darted off to investigate a group of children playing with toy cars on a mound of dirt. He halted a few yards from them and observed; then he lunged at a miniature car and *hockeyed* it.

"Go away!" The boys shooed him. Head low, tail limp, Willy trotted off, meandered a few yards, and then backtracked. He sauntered toward the boys, inching closer and closer until he towered over a little boy kneeling in the dirt. Willy opened his mouth in a pseudo-yawn, snatched the boys' ear-muffed hat right off his head, and tore down the hill. The boys chased him; their breath produced cloudlike formations as Willy beat a path to the nearby woods. When the sun slid down the side of the mountain, I heard Willy's tail thumping against the door. "Ahhroo," he barked, laying the tattered cap at my feet. Our doorstep became the depository for his many treasures.

On most days, children scuffed their shoes and swung their lunch bags as they walked down our dead-end road to school. Willy was lazy. He'd lounge out front until a group of children passed, and then he'd jump up, wag his tail wildly, and amble a few feet down the road with them. He traded dog slurps for pats on his big old head before he returned to his pallet to wait for the next group.

One day, while I was washing dishes, the vitality in his bark startled me. My heart pounded as I raced to the door and caught a glimpse of Willy rounding the bend. I hoped he was chasing an animal instead of a child. I grabbed my coat and darted after him with my nightgown flapping at my ankles. Huffing and puffing, we nearly collided head-on as Willy headed back around the bend at full speed toward home. He had a white paper bag swinging like a pendulum in his mouth.

I scolded him as I tried to catch my breath. "What do you have now? Stop, bad boy!"

Willy slowed to a trot and walked alongside me. We both collapsed on the wooden doorstep. I pried the drool-soaked bag from his jaws, peered inside, and shook my head in disbelief. I ripped the bottom from the bag and removed the contents.

"Here you go, goofy," I said, extending the stolen offering. He devoured the glazed doughnut in one gulp. When we went back inside, I poured my pregnant self a glass of milk and dunked the other one.

Winter brought short days and long, forever nights. On the evening of the school basketball tournament, it was pitch black when the parade of school buses roared by, plinking gravel at our home. When silence descended, I was wrist-deep in flour, making cinnamon rolls. I heard excited voices and rapidly approaching footsteps. An urgent pounding on the door sent me scurrying. Three breathless boys tried to talk at the same time.

"Coach needs you to come get your goofy dog."

"Yeah, he's in the gym chasing the basketball."

"And we can't start the tournament."

I jogged through the darkness, afraid of encountering wild buffalo, moose, or caribou. I heard a beastly, guttural growl and imagined a grizzly. Then I recognized the *ahhroo*. I clutched Willy's neck flab with a floured hand and my seven-months-pregnant belly with the other hand, and led the naughty boy home.

The next day, as I walked home from the post office while reading a letter, I spied a squat, white cone-shaped object on our doorstep. A toy rocket? Willy pounced on his treasure. He tossed the neighbor lady's plus-size bra, which he had yanked off her clothesline, into the air. I played tug-of-war with him, intending to return it, but he ripped off the strap. I gave the bra a dignified burial in the bottom of the community trash barrel and guiltily watched it go up in smoke when the rubbish was legally burned later that evening.

After two years of Willy's antics, townspeople were glad when my former husband's Army discharge was imminent. We arrived at the airport with Willy and his veterinarian records. They didn't have a cage big enough to transport him. Departure could not be postponed, so we sent him back with the soldier who'd purchased our home. The soldier promised to drive 100 miles back to the airport to ship Willy home the next weekend.

"Listen now, old boy, you be good. We'll see you soon," I said in farewell. Willy thumped his tail as our tears moistened the top of his head. We boarded the plane with our newborn daughter and without our big, goofy dog. We tried for days, and then weeks, to contact the soldier. There was no telephone service, and he never responded to our letters. After a month, I wrote to the neighbor whose bra Willy had stolen. I didn't apologize. I merely inquired about Willy's fate. She informed us that the weekend after we left, our home caught fire and burned to the ground. Willy had escaped but had not returned.

We never discovered what happened to Willy. I still find comfort in believing that the dazzling aurora borealis illuminated his nights and that he frolicked among the wildflowers during warm summer days. He was an expert at tipping trash barrels; I knew he'd find food until someone found him. These images, never far from my mind, consoled me.

After four decades, Willy's memory lives on. I sometimes envision a buffalo startling for no apparent reason and Willy nipping playfully at its heels. I find solace in believing that Willy's spirit roams in the land of the midnight sun as he gallivants across the Last Frontier.

LINDA O'CONNELL'S work has appeared in several *Chicken Soup for the Soul* books, magazines, newspapers, and anthologies. She and her husband, Bill, have a blended family of four adult children and nine grandchildren, ages one through nineteen, who tickle her fancy and have given her lots of "laugh" lines.

That Lion-Hearted Brother of Mine

AMRITA DATTA

Grandpa's definition of a pet was the fish in our pond, but our elder dog Pompy's good manners had won him over. Pompy was a slim, elegant mutt, jet black with streaks of white near her legs, lower back, and ears. Not long after Pompy came to live with us, our stately beauty gave birth to four little wonders and an odd little one. While the other puppies had Pompy's good looks and loved being petted and cuddled, the little one was odd-looking and feisty and recoiled from our touch. With his tiny bark and toothless gums, he would try his best to intimidate, so no one was surprised when, after seven months, he was the only one not adopted. We had to keep him, if only because he was Pompy's favorite. He had a dark, golden coat with dark, brown hair framing his face, resembling a lion's mane. In India, *Sher* means lion so, rather than pondering a deeper meaning for a special name, as is our custom, the family not so lovingly named him Sheri.

By the time Sheri was three, he had shooed away every street hawker who came within a yard of the house, snarled at Mom whenever she came home late from work (it was late for his dinner!), and bit off and spat half my uncle's moustache when he tried to teach him how to do tricks. But something changed on one ordinary day in October 1985: I was born.

Sheri is in almost every baby picture. He followed me around like a shadow. His wild days were far from over, but with me he behaved like a saint—almost, anyway. If Mom stopped rocking my cradle in the night and I cried, Sheri would put a paw on the cradle and rock me back to sleep. We grew up chasing butterflies in the backyard and digging for carrots in the vegetable garden. He loved playing horse for me, and I rode him like he really was one. We loved feeding the fish together, during which he valiantly resisted the temptation to make a meal of them. Now and again, Sheri and I would embark on great adventures. He would lure me up to forbidden territory—the attic—where we found pigeon eggs, broken kites, big wooden chests, and old family pictures! It became our secret meeting place, the treasure house we had read about in books.

Mom and Dad were separated, and for half my childhood, I had only one of my parents around. Sheri filled the gap completely. Whether it was helping me learn to ride a bicycle, cheering me while I repeatedly failed to climb the mulberry tree, or encouraging me to stand up against the bullies in the park, Sheri was always there. He even reprimanded me with a full-throttled bark if I did not finish my homework. He would keep watch while I buried the pieces of the china vase I broke, and he'd distract the family by an unusual display of histrionics while I sneaked up to my room to wash up after playing in puddles. He showed me how to bury the food I hated: fried bitter gourd, spinach, and steamed mustard fish. We found it funny when our cleaning lady discovered lumps of "weird stuff" under the carpet.

In the summer of 1993, my dad returned. My dad hated dogs, and still does. I remember pressing my nose hard against the rear window of my father's van, squinting my teary eyes to see Sheri at the gate, a paw raised in goodbye. He knew we were leaving and didn't understand why he and Pompy couldn't come with us. Unfortunately, I didn't have Sheri's indomitable spirit, his willful mind. I wasn't strong enough to stand up against my father and say, "Sheri is not an ordinary dog!" Still, Sheri wouldn't understand why I didn't fight for him, because to him, life was what *you* wanted it to be.

A year later, Pompy started showing serious signs of aging. For a while, she was bedridden, undergoing dialysis. Sheri never left her side. He would lick his mother's ears and paws, throw a fit if the doctor was late for his biweekly visit, and make sure Pompy always had a bowl of water and food, just in case she got better.

When I came to visit two summers later, long after Pompy had died, Sheri was still the same lion-hearted brother I had always known. We played, we ran, we sang, and we read books together, just as if I had never been away. When it came time to leave, I decided that it was about time Sheri's spirit had rubbed off on me. Growing up with that furry, fearless comrade had taught me a thing or two about courage. With him by my side, I begged my father to let me take Sheri home with us. As if he knew that he had to behave, Sheri did everything to tamper down his wild ways. He wiped his paws before coming into the house, resisted barking at the newspaper boy, and even resisted biting when my now clean-shaven uncle teased him for being "a good boy."

Today, Sheri's ashes lie beside Pompy's on my grandpa's farm, under the shade of the big mulberry tree he used to watch me climb. Sheri passed away peacefully in his sleep three years after we were reunited. Those three years were the best times of our lives. We built a whole new world around each other that sometimes included his spirited and fiery personality. He and my father developed a relationship of convenience, keeping out of each other's way. Sheri was—and still is—the talk of our little town, the bearer of my childhood dreams, my inspiration, and a lovely bedtime story for my little nephews and nieces, in which he will always be that lion-hearted brother of mine.

AMRITA DATTA, an engineer by profession, is currently a PhD student at the Department of Pharmacology in the School of Medicine at Tulane University. At twenty-two, she is still trying to follow in Sheri's footsteps, trying to make sure her life is what she wants it to be. Some still say growing up with Sheri spoiled her. Time will tell.

Our First Child

BILLY CUCHENS

My wife and I started trying to get her pregnant around the same time we moved into our first house. About a month later, we became parents to Lucy, a ten-pound bouncing puppy.

Shortly after Lucy came home, a debate arose between my wife and me over how our new puppy would view us. While my wife already saw herself as the matriarch of the household, I thought people who didn't have children and referred to themselves as "Mom" and "Dad" to their pets were a bit weird.

Just a few days prior, I had seen a woman walking her toy poodle in a netted stroller. At first I thought it odd to put a dog in a baby stroller, and then I realized she was actually pushing a stroller designed specifically for miniature dogs. One would assume that poodle had become the center of this woman's affection and that she had reduced herself to merely being the dog's chauffeur. This was a family dynamic I had no interest in embracing.

Still, we mulled it over for several days, and eventually my wife won me over. "What about when we have kids? We can't have the kids calling us 'Mom' and 'Dad' and the dog calling us by our first names," she said, laughing. So we became Lucy's mom and dad.

It wasn't just us. In many ways, our society embraced and encouraged humans to act as the rightful parents of their pets. At the bank, drive-through tellers kept dog biscuits next to the lollipops. Our neighborhood had a dog park next to the kids' park. One time, a drive-through ice cream shop offered us a "pup cup," a small, shallow Styrofoam cup containing vanilla custard smeared along the edges. Lucy devoured the custard and the Styrofoam cup in fifteen seconds, and we laughed for days about it.

When we selected a boarding facility for Lucy, the owner gave us a tour. "Each individual cage has its own TV which always stays on Animal Planet. The dogs get popcorn on movie night. And, by the way, we don't call ourselves a kennel. We are a Pet Spa and Resort."

The spa offered a wide range of packages. The Deluxe package included "recess" time. The Elite package offered a nature walk. The most expensive package, the VID (Very Important Dog), included a ball-throwing session with a tennis player. We were told that on movie night, they would be watching *Snow Dogs*.

When we picked Lucy up the following Monday, the spa gave us a report card which included summaries of her meal times, bath times, and other spa observations. "I was a good dog." "I enjoyed my meals." "I did not care for my nails being clipped." It was kind of fun but a bit strange to see words put in my dog's mouth, particularly in the form of self-evaluation. "I was a handful, but my hosts loved me anyway."

Although Lucy was only a few months old, she already seemed too smart for our own good. She learned the housebreaking rules in just over a week. Although she had never favored my wife or me, Lucy always seemed to obey my commands rather than hers. When we went to bed at night, my wife would tell Lucy to get on the bed several times to no avail; I'd tell her once, and she'd jump up like she had been sitting on a spring. However, as she matured, Lucy became increasingly selective about obedience. Whenever we issued a command, she would cock her head and look at us, as if considering her options. We presumed she was carefully weighing what was in it for her. Occasionally, she would pretend not to understand our command. But most of the time, she'd gamble on our impatience by hiding. She'd assume we weren't going to go to the trouble to find her and force her to complete the task. Most of the time, she was right.

Lucy effectively became our "warm-up" child. For Lucy's first Halloween, my wife bought her costume in the middle of September. By October, Lucy had outgrown it. My wife searched multiple stores for a bigger size. When she couldn't find one, she switched costumes. I'd come home from work to find Lucy wearing a loose-fitting pirate costume one day and a tight Superman costume the next day. By Halloween, my wife had purchased and returned four costumes.

She repeated the same process in November as the weather got colder and Lucy "needed" a winter coat and a Santa hat for the Christmas family portrait. "Look at your daughter, honey," my wife said as she attempted to position the dog in front of the fireplace. "Isn't she adorable next to her stocking? Is Santa going to bring Mommy's little doggie a present?" On Father's Day, my wife awakened me with breakfast in bed, a present, and two cards—one from her and one from the dog.

We bought our first kiddie pool that summer and spent countless hours relaxing in the backyard, watching Lucy sprint around and attempt to doggie paddle through three inches of water. We also childproofed the house for Lucy. And, as would occur with a first child, Lucy taught me how to roughhouse without harming her and how to control my temper when our little darling annihilated my books. She taught my wife how to take special pride in her child's appearance. One day my wife came home with horse conditioner. "I want her coat to be shiny," she said cheerily, as if this were perfectly normal. My wife also bought specialty dog food cookbooks and bone-shaped cookie cutters and spent hours in the kitchen feverishly baking low-calorie ham frittata and Santa Fe quiche, sans onions of course.

Now that my wife and I have human children, we secretly fear that we may have spent all the affection parents typically lavish upon their first child on Lucy. We do our best to disperse our love equally among all our children—human or canine—but Lucy was our first child and will always have that special place in our heart. We can only hope that our children will never wonder if they had to settle for scraps.

BILLY CUCHENS lives in the Dallas area with his two human children. Lucy is doing well, and the family now has a second canine child. Billy has written several articles for *Adoptive Families* and *Fostering Families Today*.

A Matter of Heart

CAROL PATTON

Within a month or two of bringing our American Eskimo puppy home from the pet store, my husband, Jimmy, and I realized he had a special gift. Mozart's forte wasn't in protecting us from strangers, rescuing people from burning buildings, or even pushing children out of harm's way. No, not Mozart. He answers to a higher calling. He believes he's a doctor—a cardiologist, to be exact.

While no medical diplomas hang on the wall above Mozart's bed, he does wear a white coat. We're thinking of buying him a stethoscope for his upcoming birthday. He already plays the role of doctor. He might as well look like one, too.

His one and only patient is Jimmy, who suffers from a bad heart and diabetes. Mozart is at war with Jimmy's illnesses and actually tries to heal his patient each and every day.

It began when Mozart was a puppy. He learned quickly that Jimmy wasn't big on exercise. He witnessed many days—I eventually stopped counting—where I would nag Jimmy for hours to walk on our new, high-tech, high-priced treadmill, which offers everything from aromatherapy to a cup holder for a 16-ounce soda or beer.

One evening, I stopped nagging Jimmy to exercise. Just quit altogether. Mozart eyed me with suspicion. What was I planning? What scheme was I putting into place? The clock ticked loudly as each minute passed. Mozart kept waiting for me to do something, anything, to help his pack leader get into shape. When he realized that I had finally surrendered, Mozart decided to take matters into his own paws.

Jimmy lay on the couch watching TV, as he usually does each evening. Mozart grabbed a red ball in his mouth and abruptly jumped on the couch—actually, onto Jimmy's chest, virtually pinning him down with all fours. At first, we thought Mozart's intent was simply to get Jimmy's attention. Looking back, we now know better. Jimmy has a pacemaker and defibrillator implanted in his chest. But due to a surgical complication, the defibrillator had never been tested, which had always remained a huge concern. Mozart wanted to make sure it worked.

Fortunately, for Jimmy's sake, the defibrillator wasn't activated. But Mozart was. He stared Jimmy down, continuously biting the ball in his mouth, which repeatedly released a squeaking noise. The noise grew so annoying Jimmy had no choice but to get off the couch and play ball with Mozart in our backyard.

Jimmy threw the ball several times, and Mozart chased it each time and then brought it back to him like a loyal friend. But that was just a ruse. After Jimmy threw the ball again, Mozart just sat there. So Jimmy walked from one end of our backyard to the other, picking up the ball then throwing it to the other side. After repeating this several times, Jimmy stopped playing fetch—but only after realizing a 30-pound warrior had conned him into exercising.

Mozart is, indeed, a warrior. He eagerly accepted the challenge of becoming a healer without any formal schooling or training, medical consults, or even technology to furnish critical health information. Best of all, he administers medical treatment without collecting any copays or insisting upon referrals—after all, he is a specialist of sorts—from Jimmy's primary care doctor. Mozart's medical prowess lies more in treatment, less in diagnosis. Since it's quite common for Jimmy to experience leg or foot pain, Mozart created a special treatment, a cocktail of sorts, to help increase circulation in Jimmy's legs and feet. He lies next to Jimmy, placing his left paw on top of Jimmy's right leg as if to hold it in place, scrapes off dead tissue with his bottom teeth, then licks the leg clean for about twenty minutes before proceeding on to the left leg. He meticulously examines each leg after he finishes, looking for any sign of improvement.

While Jimmy's cardiologist doesn't exactly encourage this alternative medical treatment (I think he's jealous that he didn't come up with the idea first), Mozart is convinced that he's conducting groundbreaking medical research that will eventually lead to a cure for heart disease. Who can argue? This has become a daily ritual that Mozart has faithfully performed for almost six years. He's always on time, takes this responsibility seriously, and never—ever—gives up. How many doctors can say the same about their own performance?

Mozart also holds steadfast to his beliefs, no matter what anyone—canine or human—says about his unorthodox medical practices. I often hear him make sounds when he sleeps, and I wonder what dogs dream about beyond bones and fire hydrants. But Mozart is no ordinary dog. He's a pioneer in the field of medicine. When he sleeps, he probably dreams of winning the Nobel Prize in physiology or medicine. Maybe he even dares to compare himself to Robert Jarvik, who helped develop an artificial heart, or Christiaan Barnard, who performed the first heart transplant.

Many people, including myself, could learn a lot from Mozart's do-or-die attitude. Despite the odds, he courageously battles an invisible enemy that has fiercely attacked his leader. Without any weapons or ammunition, without any troops, he enters the field of medicine alone, fighting solely with instinct to defeat his foes. He will never give up. He will never wave the white flag. What more could any human ask?

CAROL PATTON'S stories are published on websites and in national trade and consumer magazines, such as *Today's Diet & Nutrition*. As an experienced freelance writer living in Las Vegas, she says stranger things have happened. If Mozart does discover a cure, he has promised her an exclusive, which will help pave the way for other dogs to enter the medical profession.

Loyalty on Three Legs

ALLAN REGIER

A black dog ran toward us. It was pretty fast, but there was something a bit odd about the way it ran. When it ran up to us and stopped, I saw the reason. "That dog's only got three legs," I said in childish surprise. One of its hind legs was only half as long as the other and didn't reach the ground. I'd never seen anything like it.

"Somebody said he got caught in a hay mower," my dad said. "He gets along all right. It's a good dog." My dad had been working at the ranch for a month or two; my mom and little brother and I were just moving in. I was much too young to go to school, and my little brother was a year younger than me.

The three-legged dog had learned to compensate for the missing appendage and got around really well in spite of his disability. He could keep up with the horses and did everything a ranch dog was supposed to do. He immediately adopted our family and went along with anybody going out of the ranch yard, especially my little brother and me. He wasn't a constant companion like dogs in the proverbial boy-and-his-dog stories, or at least I don't remember it that way; maybe I was still too young to develop a close relationship with a pet.

The three-legged dog had been born and bred on a ranch and was a ranch dog through and through. He would start off with us and then disappear following a scent, to investigate a noise, or maybe just to check out his territory. After a while, he would come back and hang out or play for a bit, and then he'd disappear again while we played. My mother said he was protecting us, but I didn't really know what she meant when she said it. Until we moved to the ranch, my world had been a suburban lot and my grandparents' yard.

A couple of months later, my brother and I were watching a bull in one of the corrals. A calf was in the corral with the bull. The bull pushed the calf away from the hay. The calf tried to get at the hay again, and the bull snorted, put its head down, shook its horns threateningly, and took a menacing step toward the calf. The calf backed way off, looking scared and hungry.

Almost fifty years later, I can't remember if we were there because Dad was feeding the cattle or not. It doesn't matter. The bull was an object of fascination. Grown men were afraid to go near it. The day before, we had watched Dad and two other ranch hands on horseback trying to drag the roped bull back to the ranch and put it in a corral. It bucked, reared, dug in its hooves, and threw itself from side to side fighting the ropes and the weight of the horses. My dad and the other two men had to fight the bull for every inch of ground.

"That bull won't let the little cow eat," my outraged brother objected. Before I realized what he was doing, he slipped between the rails of the corral fence and was walking toward the bull.

"We're not allowed in there," I told him. "Come back." I shouted it once or twice more, but my brother ignored me.

The bull had his head down eating the hay on the ground. My brother marched straight up to that big, ferocious bull and kicked it right between the eyes. I could hardly believe it. The meanest bull on the range backed up a step or two, looked at my little brother with red mist in its eyes, put its head down, and started pawing the ground.

I knew it was going to charge. I don't think I understood what death was at that age, but I felt it encroach on some instinctive level. Then I heard barking, and from out of nowhere that three-legged dog came running up to the corral, ducked under the bottom rail at full speed, and planted itself in the space between the bull and my brother. The bull kept pawing the ground, but the dog stood its ground, barking furiously.

My three-year-old brother just stood there glaring obstinately at the bull, oblivious to what a dangerous situation he had created. The three-legged dog continued barking viciously while feinting and diving at the bull. Once or twice, he forced the bull to take a step backward, away from my brother.

"Get out of the corral. Now!" Our father's voice boomed from somewhere behind me.

My brother stopped glaring at the bull, turned, and ran for the fence. Because that three-legged dog never let up and kept the bull occupied, my brother was able to make it to the fence, where he quickly climbed out of the corral.

When the dog looked back to verify that my brother was safe, the bull lunged forward and tried to gore the three-legged dog with its horns. The dog saw, or sensed, it in time and avoided the horns, dancing out of the way on its good legs and then spinning around to face the bull. The standoff resumed for a moment, and then the three-legged dog decided his presence was no longer necessary and made a mad dash for the fence, spinning around frequently to bark at the pursuing bull to keep it at bay. The bull made a final charge at the three-legged dog just as he dove under the corral fence. The dog slid under the fence in the nick of time, and milliseconds later the bull rammed into the bottom rail, causing the whole corral to shake—and that bottom rail was a solid log well over a foot in diameter.

Almost fifty years later, I still believe the three-legged dog saved my brother's life that day, and if that's not heroic, I don't know what is.

ALLAN REGIER'S ranching experience ended before he was old enough to attend school, when his parents moved back to the suburbs. He has sometimes worked as a stock market reporter and once briefly owned a used bookstore. As this is creative nonfiction, he has not really published any fiction. That might change.

Kid Land Security

PRISCILLA CARR

My childhood mutt, Major, a black Lab mix, was a "toss-away" pup that my grandmother rescued on the street curb, in the Mission Hill District of Boston. He was a runt with a lame left leg but shining eyes and a lively personality. His face licks more than made up for his shortcomings. I was a pup myself, just reaching ten years old. I had girlfriends at school, but Major also became a friend and my regular walking companion. He was interested in everything and dug up dandelions from the sidewalk cracks and sniffed out salamis in paper bags that the women lugged from the old Haymarket Square.

Major was also a kid's service dog. He pulled me back from the street corners before a racing cab or motorcycle could clip me. He was a good judge of character, too, and steered me away from carrying the bags of a drunkard or two. Major was my protector and raised barking and howling fits to prevent me from accepting rides in neighborhood cars, even in the rain or a blizzard. He simply would not budge no matter how hard I yanked the leash or yelled. He also protested when I tried to cross the trolley tracks for a shortcut.

I was a city kid in a third-floor walk-up, yet I felt like Wendy Darling from *Peter Pan* with her Saint Bernard, Nana, as a nanny. People remarked on Major's shining coat and piercing eyes. When Major and I strutted on those sidewalks, I felt like somebody. I loved to answer the kids' questions:

"Is he yours?"

"Where'd ya get him?"

"What kind is he?"

That summer I became ill with rheumatic fever and the mumps. For five weeks, Major sat all day curled up next to me on the bed and whimpered when I was in pain. Friends' visits dwindled, but Major's attentions never diminished. From sixth to eighth grade, as a result of rheumatic fever, I suffered from repeated throat infections and joint and muscle pain. Reading and listening to rock-and-roll on my RCA record player and transistor radio replaced softball and sock hops in the church basement. I chose stories Major and I would enjoy, such as *Lassie Come Home* and *Black Beauty*. I actually read out loud to him and sought his opinions.

"Do you think Lassie will make it, boy?"

"How can anyone treat Beauty so cruelly?"

He asserted with a "Woof!" or cocked his head and pondered. I whispered in his ear at bedtime, "Can't wait to see what will happen next," and Major jumped excitedly, his tongue hanging out. I was sure he understood everything I read and that he answered my questions. Dad once overheard me reading to Major and muttered, "She thinks that dog can understand her." Adults can be so dumb.

When my throat seared and my fever spiked, pain relief came from a wet nose on my neck and that lame, little body curled up next to me. Tail wags and face licks made me happy. Major and I shared similar tastes in food. I stopped asking for peanut butter and tuna sandwiches, because it was clear Major preferred baloney and cheese and deviled ham. I would open my Roy Rogers lunchbox halfway and ask, "What have we got, boy?" And Major would woof joyously. If we got Hostess Twinkies, I teased him by sticking a dollop of pasty, fake cream on his nose and laughed while watching him lick it off. He was adorable when he teetered on his hind legs and "arfed" like a seal, trying to catch my Cracker Jacks on his tongue. Nobody had more fun than we did. Gran once passed my bedroom, and when she heard me cackling and Major howling, asked, "What on earth is going on in there?" Before I could answer, she crossed herself and pleaded, "May the saints preserve us!" and proceeded to feather dust and sweep the hallway.

There was much discussion about having a dirty dog on my bed. The sight of it sickened my father, and he complained, "How can Priscilla get better with that filthy fleabag on her bed?" Imagine if he'd known Major and I kissed each other.

My grandmother stuck up for Major and told Dad, "He makes her happy. She'd be sicker without him." She also scrubbed Major in the bathtub every Saturday and massaged him with flea powder.

My family almost gave Major away that fall. The Rooney girls and Tommy Maloney and I decided we could transfer our sidewalk hopscotch skills to hopping or jumping rooftops between the triple-decker apartment buildings. We had watched the older kids do it. I hitched Major's leash to a small clothesline post. Annie Rooney leapt first and cleared it easily. She was the tallest. Tommy went next and had about a foot to spare on landing, which made me gulp because he was a bit taller than me. Major became increasingly agitated and began barking nonstop.

We had lined up by height, which meant Maureen was next. When she hesitated, we heckled by clucking and taunting, "Whatssa matter, ya chicken?" She ran off, and we laughed. Now, it was up to me. I was wearing my new Keds, advertised to add "wings" to my feet, so there was no bailing out. As I backed up to get my head start for the leap, Major went wild, howling like a wolf. He twisted and pulled and broke the metal clip that connected the leash to the collar, and he immediately sank his teeth through my Wrangler jeans and into my calf. Blood spurted. It was the worst pain I had ever felt.

Tommy pulled Major away and said, "Has he gone nuts with rabies or somethin'?"

A neighbor hollered up, "Get down from there, you kids."

I ran home, and Grandmother poured hydrogen peroxide and mercurochrome on the bite and bandaged my leg. "That dog will have to go, and that's that," she declared, plopping me on my bed and laying an ice pack on my leg before chaining Major to the back porch.

When my parents got home, the family round table started, with me in the hot seat. I cracked fast and spilled it—the whole truth and nothing but the truth. How could I let Major take the heat on this one? They sat staring at me, speechless. My grandmother wiped perspiration from her face, and Mom went as pale as Casper. Finally, Dad said, "That fleabag saved her life."

Another long couple of minutes passed, and then Dad said, "Unchain the mutt and bring him in."

We never spoke of it again. I didn't even get the switch.

PRISCILLA CARR also wrote about Major's surprising puppy rescue in *A Cup of Comfort® for Dog Lovers*. Her story about her lively and eccentric sixth-grade teacher, Miss Cotter, appeared in *My Teacher Is My Hero*. Priscilla's behavioral-medicine writing appears in psychological and medical journals. Richard, her husband of forty years, is her Ever Muse.

Jack and the Mud Pies

JOYCE L. RAPIER

*S*tay, Jack! Don't you move, because I'll be right back. Those words thundered through my head as images of Jack danced inside my mind. I caught a glimpse of a young child, running between tall Johnson grasses—flowing long-blond hair trailing in the wind—stopping abruptly to try to catch a willful Monarch butterfly. *Jack, I told you to stay. Now, look what you did! I missed my butterfly. It's okay, Jack, I love you. Let's go back and check our mud pies.*

Jack's tail would whip frantically as we pranced together, following our trail back to the duck pond. We checked our pies and went to the back door. As I pounded as hard as a four-year-old child could and as Jack barked, Mother came running to the door. "What's the matter? Are you hurt?"

"No, Momma, I need a spoon and a Mason jar full of water."

"You two scared the daylights out of me. I don't mind giving you the spoon, but there's a whole duck pond full of water. Why don't you scoop up the water in your tin cup?"

"No! You know how Jack loves the water. He makes ripples and splashes me."

"You could stand a little water on your dirty face. What on earth have you been doing?"

"Making mud pies."

"Well, you look like you have been wallowing in pig slop. Look at your face!"

"I can't see my face. Aren't you going to scold Jack? He's dirty, too."

"Dogs get dirty, but I must admit—Jack needs a bath. What have you done to Jack?"

"Nothin'. I told you we have been making mud pies."

I took the spoon and water from Mother, and Jack and I soon made our way to the duck pond. The pies we had made earlier that morning were baking nicely in the sun, so the two of us lay together on the green grass. Jack and I talked about everything: how the clouds made funny faces, about birds, snakes and bees, and why he was getting old. Jack seemed tired for several weeks but never whimpered or gave way to pain.

Jack was the most beautiful German shepherd with a brindle muzzle, huge, brown eyes, a brown face, and a sleek, black body. He wasn't a dog. He was my companion and my hero, and we went everywhere together. We seemed to be joined at the hips.

Many times, Jack would allow me to ride him like a horse and then stop and toss me off his back. He would stand over me like a giant, explaining to me not to hold on to his ears, and then he'd sit down and let me climb upon his back. He was my protector, guarding me with the fiercest growl when a stranger came into the yard, and he more than once took stance in defending his domain.

Jack, my sweet Jack, was getting old, and I couldn't understand why he couldn't live forever. Why, fifteen years wasn't old! Our conversation ended and we lay there basking in the sun, until it was time to make more mud pies. Instinctively, Jack made his way to the duck pond, with me in hot pursuit, my short legs trying to keep up with the four-legged love of my life. He sat down at the edge of the pond and waited for me to catch up, looking at me as if to say, *See there, I beat you again!*

I retrieved my old mixing bowl from the ground and shook out all the caked mud from its interior. Slowly, I placed sifted dirt inside the bowl, added water and a secret ingredient—rotten duck eggs. Jack sat so patiently, looking at the dark chocolate mud—waiting, waiting—knowing he would get the first taste of our newly concocted batch of mud pies.

"Ya ready, boy?" Jack looked at me as his tongue lapped and drooled for the anticipated delight. When I was too slow in spooning out his portion, Jack would nudge me on the legs as if to say, *What's the problem? Can't you see I need a bite? Get on with it.*

At last, the pies were ready to taste and Jack held the stiffened mud pie between his teeth and chomped with gusto. He would spit and sputter as mud caked his muzzle, and then he'd sneeze until his entire face was dripping wet with duck egg goop and mud. His eyes would squint as though he were eating sour pickles, and then without warning, he would jump into the duck pond to expunge the rotten taste inside his mouth. It never failed. I was the one who got the bath as he shook muddy water, duck feathers and residue my way. It didn't matter, he laughed—as dogs do laugh. It was his way of getting back at me for making him sit there and eat that stuff. Summer was wonderful, and my childhood was gifted in so many ways—compliments of Jack.

Several months passed and winter was closing in on our little world. An early snow blanketed the ground, and large footprints etched the crusty ground. As I peered through the window in anticipation of making snow angels and eating Mom's delicious snow ice cream, my heart was sad. There were no dog prints—no Jack prints—just my daddy's. Running from window to window, I watched as Daddy went to the toolshed, took out a shovel and prepared a cold grave near the duck pond. My world came crashing to the ground.

Painfully, I watched my beloved companion being laid to rest. Tears bolted from my eyes, and I rushed outside, oblivious to obstacles in my path. Barefooted, I stood there completely frozen—unable to say a word. Daddy, seeing and feeling my pain, cradled me into his arms. He walked over to the place where Jack and I made the mud pies, lifted some of the dried pies from a protected shelf, and handed them to me.

Kneeling into the freshly fallen snow, I placed the mud pies upon Jack's grave, told him I loved him, and said good-bye. Thank you, Jack. I will forever remember those childhood memories of mud pies and you—my wonderful friend, companion, confidant, and hero.

JOYCE L. RAPIER has had two short stories, *Hidden Wings* and *Messy Kisses*, published in *Chicken Soup for the Father and Daughter Soul* and *Chicken Soup for the Soul, a Tribute to Moms*. She currently writes short, memorable stories for her local newspaper, the *Press Argus Courier*.

Cleo Saves the Day

PEG RYAN

She came to us by default. No one in our tiny collection of houses in the woods wanted her, so despite the protestations of my animal-resistant husband, she came to live with us. Her name was Cleo, a beagle-basset mix with the dwarflike legs of a basset and the body and dreamy eyes of a beagle.

I can't be sure what thoughts lay behind those dreamy eyes when she met her new family, but she seemed amenable. We were a family of four—Mom, Dad, and a set of year-and-a-half-old twin girls, who might have sent some dogs running back to the nearest animal shelter. Luckily, Cleo stayed.

Like most hunting breeds, Cleo loved to be outside. Most times we found her basking in the sun on top of a pile of fallen oak leaves. She never ventured far from home. I sometimes wondered why she didn't wander away, but I've come to believe that Cleo didn't quite trust our parenting skills. She would never leave our children.

When I would load our girls into the stroller for a walk, Cleo always walked with us, positioning herself between the stroller and the few cars that would appear on the dirt road. As the girls grew older and began visiting with friends, Cleo was never out of visual contact. She would find a patch of sun near the playing children and settle in on her stakeout.

About two years after Cleo adopted us, our family grew with the arrival of a son, Christopher. Cleo seemed delighted with the new arrival, sleeping beside his crib or near his tiny infant seat on the floor. If he woke up, Cleo would pad into the kitchen to announce, with a bark, his awakening. When he would coo or even spit up, I was summoned to his side by a whine.

Cleo seemed quite content with her role as nanny to our three children. When they were outside playing, she was with them, ever vigilant. When inside, she took a well-deserved rest, but always within sight of the kids.

Cleo experienced real trauma when the girls began school. On their first day, we all walked to the bus stop—Leah, Shawna, Christopher, Cleo, and me. The big, yellow bus rumbled to a stop and the girls, excited beyond all reason, climbed on, followed closely by a little brown and white dog with stumpy legs. Cleo could barely make the jump onto the bus, but—in her little mind—the girls were not going without her.

The bus driver was unimpressed with our dog's display of loyalty to her kids, but Cleo would not get off even when commanded to do so. Finally, the girls jumped off long enough for Cleo to follow behind them, and I held the dog while they reboarded the bus. It rumbled off, leaving a very distressed Cleo squirming in my grasp.

After several weeks of this daily bus-stop struggle with Cleo, my daughters informed us that they no longer needed an escort to the corner. Since I could see their walk to the bus from my back door, I agreed to stay behind. Cleo was not so easily persuaded.

On the first day solo, I kissed them goodbye, with tears in my eyes, and then ran to the back door, where Christopher and I could watch them. Shortly thereafter, I realized that someone was missing—Cleo had escaped to follow them. About fifteen minutes later, she ambled up the driveway and into the house. Ten minutes after Cleo returned, I received a phone call from the school. Cleo had been banished from the bus stop. She did not take it well and remained distraught, frequently trying to sneak behind the girls as they left. Slowly she recovered, refocusing all her impressive parenting skills on Christopher.

While the girls were in school, Chris, now two, and I tried to coax mums to grow in the sandy soil of the pine barrens. Each morning, Chris, Cleo, and I would troop outside, armed with potting soil, an assortment of garden tools, gallons of plant food, some tiny trucks, and a pint-sized shovel. While I dug, pruned, prayed over, fed, and watered a few scraggy mums, Chris would sit on the ground and push his trucks through the sand. Cleo would take her position on a pile of leaves and doze in the autumn sun. It was a pleasurable time for all of us, so pleasurable that perhaps I became a bit complacent. After all, Chris never strayed—until he did.

We were all doing our usual jobs. After a few minutes at my task, in the recesses of my plant-addled mind, I realized that something was wrong. I glanced quickly around the yard. Chris was gone. My two-year-old son had wandered off. Thousands of horrible visions flashed like fireworks. My panic level rose with each shout until tears blinded my vision and breathing was almost impossible.

I ran to the front of the house, but Christopher was nowhere in sight. I ran back, calling his name, screaming for him. A sound pierced through my terror. It was Cleo, loudly barking and growling. I began running toward the sound coming from our neighbor's horse corral. Two gigantic horses resided in that pen. As I approached, I saw my little guy standing right in the middle, calling the horses. Fear for his life was quickly supplanted with relief crashing over me. Through my tear-swollen eyes, I spied the giant horses huddled against the back of the fence, their eyes wide open with fear. Jumping and barking near their deadly hooves was our little brown and white dog with stumpy legs.

Cleo kept the horses at bay until I retrieved Christopher from the pen. As soon as we cleared the fence, Cleo ceased her din and ran out of the pen with more speed than I ever thought she possessed.

The horses are now gone, along with the horse pen. The toddler is now thirty-one years old, and Cleo has long since gone to her rest. Once in a while, I look at the place where the horse pen stood and remember that day, that terror, and how my heroic little brown and white dog with the stumpy legs saved the day. I like to imagine Cleo sitting on a pile of leaves somewhere, basking in the sun.

PEG RYAN is a mother of three. By profession, she was a teacher for thirty-one years and is now retired. In her retirement, she spends a great deal of time with her three grandsons and directing a choir in her church.

Brownie: Mrs. Campbell's Electrified Dog

BILL CHEW

One summer day, during the Depression, my new puppy, Four Spot, arrived. I happily prepared him a bed on our front porch, petted him, and made him comfortable. In a short time, the dogs in the neighborhood came to welcome him. A main feature of their welcoming was to mark their territory. This involved lifting a rear leg and sprinkling on the side of our house, just outside the screen door. There were several dogs, and they made repeated welcoming visits.

In a matter of days, we had a host of flies buzzing around our screen door. Whenever we opened the door, large green flies entered, eager to migrate to the kitchen. Mama couldn't stand a fly in her house, let alone a large, green, ugly fly in her kitchen. She decreed that it was my dog and thus my problem to solve, quickly. In the meantime, I was to mop the front porch, daily.

Chasing the visiting dogs did no good—they viewed it as a game and returned as soon as I went into the house. Then it occurred to me that if farmers used electric fences to keep cattle in, why couldn't I invent an "electric fence" to keep dogs away?

It took a short while to locate some screen wire in the garage. At the site of the most sprinkled area, I tacked a good-sized piece of the screen to the porch floorboards and another piece to the side of the house too high for my puppy to reach. If a dog sidled up to this preferred spot and stood on the screen on the floor, a circuit would be completed when he sprinkled on the screen tacked to the side of the house. I was pleased with my brilliance.

My friend Gene Camplain came by to help with the design. We used the two wires from our 110-volt house current. One wire went "through" a light bulb and on to the floor screen. The other went through a light bulb and on to the other screen. It was our thinking that the light bulbs would absorb most of the shock and the dog would receive a very mild but uncomfortable jolt.

We were eager to try out our invention but needed a dog. The Campbell family lived a block east of us on White Street and their dog, Brownie, was a frequent and voluminous offender. Gene hit on the idea that, if he went home (he lived across the street from the Campbells) and returned using a shortcut, Brownie would follow. Sure enough, here came Gene with Brownie following along. Brownie was a medium-sized, short-haired "galoot" of a dog. He was happy-go-lucky, liked everyone, and had a long tail that wagged continuously.

Brownie hopped up on our porch, approached the favored corner, sniffed thoroughly, hiked up a back leg, and let fly. Neither Gene, nor I, nor Brownie was prepared for what happened next. Brownie laid back his ears and let out a loud and painful yelp. On his first leap, his toenails gained traction on the screen wire attached to the floor, and he covered quite a distance. But the porch had recently been painted with high-gloss "Battleship Gray" deck enamel, so he had trouble on the smooth surface. There was a great deal of toenail scratching and leg flailing as he seemed to be running at high speed but advancing slowly. Finally, he scrambled off the porch and ran full tilt for home.

Across the street from our house was a vacant lot where we could see the back of the Campbells' house. We watched in stunned silence as Brownie—yelping all the way—tore across the lot, into his backyard and around the side yard. An ominous silence followed.

Gene and I began to have second thoughts. After all, we liked Brownie and hadn't meant to inflict real pain. We worried that we might have electrocuted him, but Gene decided that was probably not the case since the last we saw of him he was running "pretty good." It then came to us that it would be a good idea to dismantle the invention, which we did immediately. Then, guilt and worry got the better of us. We decided to go to Gene's house and, on the way, saunter by the Campbells' house to see about Brownie.

Since Brownie had come from the direction of my house, we knew that if we came from the same direction we would be immediate suspects. Cleverly, we thought, we approached from a roundabout way. We barely had turned the corner when we had been sighted. We couldn't turn back without, in effect, admitting guilt, so we strolled on, as nonchalantly as we could.

Mrs. Campbell was on her front porch consoling Brownie, who was licking first one leg and then the other, looking pathetic. Upon spotting us, Mrs. Campbell said, "Billy Chew, what have you done to my dog?" We hastily denied doing anything, anytime, whatever it was. Unfortunately, at the sound of our voices, Brownie, the traitor, let out a frantic yelp and ran under the porch.

"Don't you two lie to me," Mrs. Campbell demanded. "Trot yourselves over here." Gene immediately cracked and confessed. He left it up to me to explain, as best I could, what we had done. I tried to give the story a positive slant. When Mrs. Campbell finally understood about the problem with the puppy and my homemade electric fence, she laughed long and hard. She said she wasn't mad at us, but she was worried about Brownie.

Gene and I sought to make amends. We got down on our knees, looked under the porch where we saw Brownie still licking away. We called in a friendly voice but, upon hearing us, he let out a long, mournful cry and retreated to the darkest recess. All we could see were the whites of his eyes.

When Dad got home that evening, I confessed everything. He said he would discuss my invention with me later, after he had visited the Campbells to see how Brownie was coming along. Brownie had emerged hale and hearty, had eaten a huge supper, and was his old dopey self. Mr. and Mrs. Campbell thought the whole episode was hilarious, and Dad returned home chuckling. He suggested that, in the future, I think a little more about the consequences of my actions.

Fate can be unexpectedly kind to two small boys. We escaped parental wrath. At our age, that was quite an accomplishment.

By some mysterious canine communication system, Brownie solved the dog problem. He passed the word, "Stay off that Battleship Gray front porch." And they did.

No more flies. This made Mama happy.

No more mopping. This made me happy.

And in my eyes, Brownie became a hero.

BILL CHEW grew up in Shirley, Indiana, a small town noted for its two tomato-canning factories (one on the east end, one on the west), two railroads, one water tower, two bars, and seven churches. Bill served in the U.S. Air Force as a pilot during World War II, earned a PhD from Purdue University, and spent his career at General Motors in Detroit. He is now retired and has returned to Indiana, where he lives with his wife, Jean, and they enjoy visits from their six children and thirteen grandchildren.

A Knight in Furry Armor

ROBERT PAUL BLUMENSTEIN

I had the honor of adopting a beautiful pair of miniature schnauzers named Otto and Hannah. My wife, Ann, and I adopted Otto first, and then we set about our task of finding him a suitable mate. We wanted them fairly close in age so they would experience puppyhood together and grow into adults as a bonded pair and not merely as a "mated" pair. Since Otto arrived first, we had to meticulously research each female candidate's pedigree to make sure her and Otto's bloodlines had not crossed. At last, our quest led us to a suitable match.

Otto accompanied us to meet his potential mate. Hannah pushed the litter's other three pups aside, waddled forward, and clambered onto me. She slathered me with puppy licks and then admonished me for taking so long to show up to take her home. So, we settled up and left in our truck, a complete family now—well almost. Otto would have nothing to do with Hannah. He absurdly moved to the farthermost point in the cab to get away from this "thing" that had so thoroughly captured the attention of his mommy and daddy. When we arrived home, Otto naturally resisted sharing his space with Hannah. Fortunately, Otto soon realized that he had a new playmate and a lifelong companion. We all bonded as a family in no time.

When Hannah experienced her first heat, she seemed surprised and Otto curious. Ann and I probably added to the mystery when we isolated them from each other, employing that marvelous invention: the child gate. When both dogs exhibited a strong desire to mate, we awaited Hannah's next heat with great anticipation.

Six months later, our dogs had mated and Hannah was "with pups." Shortly before she whelped, we took her to the veterinarian to make sure there would be no complications and that her health was not in danger. The doctor gave her two thumbs up. Right before we left the examination room, the vet asked us if we wanted to board Otto with him for a couple of weeks after Hannah had whelped. Ann and I were completely dumbfounded. He explained that Otto might sneak in and kill the puppies. I certainly couldn't imagine what he was talking about. I had heard of lions and baboons behaving like this, but a dog, my dog?

We politely thanked the doctor for his concern and assured him that we would exercise all due caution by keeping an eye on Otto throughout the whole process, and that boarding Otto with him during this very special time was completely out of the question. After all, we were family!

Soon after, Hannah delivered four beautiful, healthy pups. Ann played midwife (although I have no idea where she gained those skills) while I metaphorically passed out cigars and Otto peered through the mesh of the child gate, his tail wagging like a metronome. I thought it best, however, to wait until the puppies had at least opened their eyes before introducing them to their dad.

We had erected a steel puppy pen around the box, locking the puppies in and Otto out. When the puppies matured enough to explore their whelping box, we brought Otto into the room to meet his brood. When the puppies scurried over to meet their daddy, Otto backed up. *Uh-oh*, I thought. Of course, they were only interested in finding a teat on his underside. I assured him it was okay, and he clicked off a few wags of his tail.

Soon after, since Otto had not displayed a single act of aggression toward the puppies, we removed the puppy pen. Otto dutifully made several visits a day to his pups. One day, after the puppies gobbled down their gruel, I observed the most tender and gentle deed ever performed by a dog. The puppies ebulliently bounced over to Otto, climbed on the side of the whelping box, and allowed Otto to lick their faces as clean as a whistle. Well, I'm not stupid. I know why he was there. He was a dog, for crying out loud. I'm sure the gruel was quite a treat for Otto. Yet something else was taking place: A special bond was forming.

When it came time to introduce the puppies to the outdoors, we experienced slight trepidation over allowing Otto to be present. Yet again, we were wonderfully surprised by his exceptional behavior. He stayed right with the pups and guarded them closely. We had a pond behind the house that attracted blue herons that swooped over the backyard upon their descent and cast formidable shadows across the lawn. On this particular day, when that very thing occurred, Otto leapt to his feet, barked, and growled fiercely at the passing aquatic predator. "Don't even think of coming near my puppies if you value your life," would be the closest translation of his barks.

Though schnauzers are not known for their herding instincts, Otto exhibited a full array of just that. If a puppy would stray too far from the play area, he would rush over and nudge the little guy or gal back into the group. Then he'd find a stick the right size for the tiny puppy and offer it up for play. Otto was accustomed to dragging huge limbs from the woods and playing with them by himself. Yet somehow, he knew that only small sticks best suited these tiny, frail creatures. Otto never once growled at the puppies, even when they explored his underside in search of a teat.

Hannah benefited from Otto's unusual parenting skills as well. Once she had done her nursing duty and the puppies came to rely on their gruel for sustenance, Hannah was decidedly finished with nursing. She was back to being an everyday dog: chasing mice in the woods, making sure birds understood the purpose of a fence, and all the other daily activities that she had engaged in before this group of midgets had shown up. Hannah considered weaning the first order of business to getting back on track. So, when Otto stood ready to offer his babysitting services, she couldn't have been happier.

I was amazed by all the wonderful things Otto did for those puppies. There could not have been a gentler, more devoted dad around. And Otto demonstrated this selfsame behavior time and time again toward all the puppies from Hannah's subsequent four litters. It was no surprise that each time a puppy was adopted and left to join its new family, Otto experienced malaise for a day or two. I couldn't help but wish that all "deadbeat dads" would learn a lesson in familial compassion from Otto. If they could have witnessed his ever-present, compassionate nurturing, they would have seen, as Hannah and I did, that Otto was nothing short of a knight in furry armor.

ROBERT PAUL BLUMENSTEIN resides in Midlothian, Virginia, with his miniature schnauzer, Fitzgerald, and his wife, Ann. He is thrilled to be included in *My Dog Is My Hero* after recently having two stories published in *Dogs: Heart-Warming, Soul-Stirring Stories of Our Canine Companions*. He also had a story published in *Woodstock Revisited: 50 Far Out, Groovy, Peace-Loving, Flashback-Inducing Stories from Those Who Were There*. Check out his latest novel, *Snapping the String*, and other published work at *www .robertblumenstein.com*.

The Bluebirds of Fife

JOYCE STARK

My husband, Eric, was seven when his family moved from Methil, in the Scottish county of Fife, across the River Tay to Dundee. Although he was young, Eric has very distinct memories of those early days in his life. Fife had been a rural county, where all his friends lived, and Dundee was a big city, where, apart from his aunts and uncles, everyone was a total stranger.

In those early days, the only thing that made life bearable for Eric was his greatest pal—his dog, Roy, a cross between a collie and an Alsatian. Eric was just over a year old when Roy turned up on their doorstep, one dark, cold rainy night in Methil. Eric's mum had heard a howling outside, and when she opened the door, there stood Roy, soaking wet and grossly underfed. They adopted him immediately!

As the move approached, Eric had often confided in Roy how reluctant he was to move away from his home. Once settled in

Dundee, during his first days at school, Eric often stood on the playground, staring longingly across the River Tay to the road that runs between Tayport and Newport in Fife. The river was the separating line, and the road he could see in the distance represented Fife to Eric, the home he had not wanted to leave. He would peer through the railings at the distant cars and buses. He couldn't discern the colors of the buses, but he knew in his mind's eye that they were the "Bluebirds" of Fife. They seemed a million miles away.

School became something Eric got through so he could rush home to Roy—the one thing that remained constant in his life. Eric wasn't interested in making new friends; Roy knew all his secrets and licked his face when he shed tears over the loss of his beloved Fife. Nevertheless, Eric marveled at how easily Roy adjusted to his new surroundings. When Eric was at school, Roy gallivanted around until he knew it was time for Eric to come home. On weekends, Roy glued himself to Eric's side, and they would play games and keep each other company. He was such a warm, likeable dog that he attracted kids. While Eric struck up conversations and began to make friends, Roy would take off to sniff other kids and join in their games. Roy became such a part of whatever was going on that the kids always included him in their games, as if he were just one of the boys.

Roy was a superaffectionate, intelligent dog, but he did like to roam! Annie Burke, a lifelong friend of Eric's mum, lived a few doors down the street. Roy knew her well, and more than once she arrived at Grimmonds Jute Mill, where she worked as a weaver, and suddenly felt a wet nose sniffing her leg. Roy had followed her straight into the factory, which meant she had to ask for time off to take Roy home.

When, after a few months, Eric and his family moved three miles outside Dundee City Centre, Roy would venture into the city on his own. People used to dodge up alleyways when they saw him coming, because, if he spotted someone he knew, he would tag on to them and follow them around, darting in and out of shops or waiting at the curb until they emerged. On his way home on the school bus, Eric would often spot Roy headed home from the city. Using a special whistle they had devised as a code, Eric would lure Roy over to the bus so he could bound alongside all the way home.

One night the local police showed up at Eric's door to report that Roy was being held in "protective custody" in a Fife police station. Eric's father had to catch a bus into Dundee and then walk down to the docks where the ferryboat sailed over to Fife. (There was no Tay Bridge in those days, so you had to cross the river by ferry.) Once in Fife, Eric's father had to catch another bus to Methil to pick up Roy. He was astounded that Roy had made his way back there on his own. It was only when he boarded the ferry to return that first one crew member and then another came up to speak to Roy. Roy would wag his tail at them, and they would say, "Hello boy, you back again?"

It turned out that Roy regularly crossed back and forth on the ferry. The crew would watch him attach himself to people, usually someone traveling solo. Roy would march behind them onto the boat and then off again on the other side, so everyone assumed he belonged to someone. On the night Eric's father fetched Roy, they asked, "So, are you his real owner?"

At least twice more Eric's father was summoned back to Fife. One of the police officers even offered to adopt Roy, if they ever wanted to part with him! Eric theorized that like him, Roy missed Fife, and Eric would often dream that the two of them would one day run off, hop the ferry, and live together in Fife—where they belonged. Their love of their early home bonded them so solidly together that Eric's mum would automatically say, "Are you two ready for your tea?" or, "Come on you two, it's time for bed."

More than fifty years have passed, and yet sometimes—when we are in Dundee—Eric will stand and gaze across the river to the road between Tayport and Newport in Fife. He still experiences that same strong ache inside that he used to get staring through the railings of Ann Street School. Eric can drive across the bridge any time he wants, but sometimes, if he concentrates really hard, he thinks he can make out the old "Bluebirds" as they head off into Fife . . . and then hear, like an echo on the breeze, the sound of Roy barking as he runs alongside the bus.

JOYCE STARK lives in northeast Scotland. Since retiring from local government, she writes about her travels in the United States and her friends and family. She describes her mind as similar to O'Hare Airport—with ideas landing, taking off, and circling overhead waiting to land!

The Chase

JESSICA BARMACK

To be fair, it's not easy to keep a dog alive. I realized this when Sam ran over that stone wall, the cord tied to her choke collar like a noose. Horrified, I walked to the edge of the drop-off, five or six feet, expecting to find my new, rescued, four-year-old Lab dangling by her neck, tongue lolling out of her mouth, eyes bulging. My eyes adjusting to the dark, I peered over the wall and found Sam stretched out on her toes, taut on the chain, embarrassed but happy to see me.

We had the yard fenced in.

A week or so later, she ran out onto Lake Rico, onto ice maybe three inches thick, unsuitable for vehicles or people or anything, except, perhaps, one smallish black Lab. Her weight equally distributed over four short legs touching down lightly as she bounded silently away, she became smaller and smaller until just a speck, closer to the island than my shore. The adrenalin coursed pointlessly through my arteries. The deep grinding of shifting ice disturbed the quiet; a leviathan moan followed by an echoed ping shot across my hearing like an arrow. Sam stopped, seemed momentarily frozen, listened, held her breath. From where she stood, I was invisible, until I moved, waving my arms, shouting. My voice blasted across the ice like buckshot. Finally, Sam decided to race back to me, after a moment's deliberation, a choice between loyalty and freedom.

Another winter, another lake: Sam galloping straight across thin ice. In she went. I, lightheaded, called to her as she struggled. Kicking madly, she got her elbows up. A resident swan honked and nipped at her backside, screamed encouragement, flapped, honked, and splashed, a smear of furious feathers. A smudge of glistening-wet black fur emerged, finally, above sickly, colorless water onto bright blue-white-gold glimmering ice.

It's hard to keep a dog alive, especially a high-spirited one with more courage and enthusiasm than sense, occupied by the pleasure of speed, velvet ears flapping in the breeze.

By the age of nine, Sam had quieted down enough to spend ten weeks of bed rest beside me during my pregnancy. She distracted me from my worries and left me only for her walks and meals. I missed her when she went out and looked forward to the padda-pat-pat of paws on stairs as she dashed back up to my room.

Sam survived Lyme disease twice.

She survived a spleenectomy and a suspicious mass that was benign.

Rimadyl was used for Sam's arthritis, when it became so painful she hadn't wanted to get up.

I used to say that I could handle Sam's death if she managed to live to be thirteen. I just wanted her to grow old and lead a good life. Then, I said, I could handle it when it came her time. But then she kept *not* dying, and I came to believe that she was immortal.

On Wednesday morning, I picked her up at the vet's office, where she had been bagged and wrapped up in a clean quilt. For our last trip together, we drove to the pet crematorium north of Madison. The technician called me ma'am, with military bearing and a Southern accent. His name was Dan. Dan cut open the plastic bag like an emergency room nurse scissoring the clothes off a patient. On the table, Sam's dark eyes open, her nose wet and cold, I patted her head and tried to absorb the fact that she was dead, not just cold, but really dead.

Gingerly and not without tenderness, Dan lifted Sam and placed her inside the roaring maw of the furnace. Designed for people and used on horses, my fifty-nine-pound dog was a light snack for the incinerator. In two hours, her charred and dehydrated remains were spread out on a tray to cool, a rocky beach strewn with broken shells. Porous marrow reduced to coral and sea sponge; teeth and debris now sand, rocks, pebbles.

I sifted through the remains and picked up bone fragments, rolling them in my fingers—shells and sea glass; a knee joint, white and almost weightless, curved like a cello; and a piece of skull, the elusive knob on the top of her head that I could never draw correctly. I put these in a plastic zip-lock bag and let Dan pulverize the rest.

Driving away, I patted the lid. I picked up the box to feel its weight in my lap. I would look over my shoulder to where Sam would be if she were not in the box.

How was I going to manage? Sam had fended off a tendency toward depression. Surely, now, grief would lead to despondency. Already, things were becoming slow and disjointed, like music shattered into random notes.

Before she died, Sam had begun to ignore me, to wean me of her constant ministrations. She encouraged our younger dog to attend to me, but Bart, a Rottweiler-shepherd, didn't go in for emotional work. Security was his detail. Moreover, he wouldn't venture across a slippery hardwood floor to see if I happened to be sniffling.

So, I found Sam wherever she was, patted her, kissed her cheek, and cried. With my bottomless emotional needs, I stressed out an exhausted elderly dog who had grown brittle with arthritis, gnawed on like a bone by cancer.

Nice.

She would have been proud to know that I was unselfish enough to end her misery as I did. But had I really considered the difficulty of surviving the death of this dog?

Sam, show me what happiness looks like.
Sam, show me what freedom looks like.
Sam, show me what forgiveness looks like.
Sam, show me what loyalty looks like.

Thirteen years go by quickly. A dog's long life is short. The end is always almost within sight, a barely visible black speck, way far away in the future, but bounding, at top speed with short legs on thin ice, toward me.

JESSICA BARMACK'S short story "Fishing Piranha" was a finalist in the 2005 New Letters competition. Her ten-minute play, *Old Friends*, was read on stage at the 2002 Herring Run Arts Festival in southeastern Massachusetts. Jessica is a freelance editor and writer.

Huckleberry, the Unlikely Hero

ALLISON PATTILLO

As far as heroes go, Huckleberry was far from standard issue. He wasn't tall and dark, although I must admit he was handsome; he wasn't brave, tough, stoic, or even athletic for that matter; he had bad knees and tended to be a bit on the chubby side; and he never saved us from a harrowing situation. But from the moment my husband picked him up at the airport, as a gift from my godmother, Huck was unabashedly ours.

Huck proved so high maintenance, from the very beginning, that we clung to the idea that he was sent to us to accomplish great things. At least this was the rationalization I concocted after I had worn out the tried and true saying "You get what you pay for."

The trials and tribulations started on the drive home. By the third time my husband called to complain about Huck's incessant wailing, he had gone from "our dog" to "your dog." This adorable puppy with the deep, soulful eyes—his saving grace—wouldn't have an accident all day. But when it came time for bed, he had to go every hour, and amazingly enough, no one else in my house could hear him when he cried. I walked around our neighborhood more with that dog than I ever did pacing in the evenings when our girls were babies.

Huck also frequently threw up during the night. At the first sounds of heaving, I rocketed out of bed so I could usher Huck outside in time. However, my jumping up, turning on lights, and yelling for him to get outside would invariably frighten him, which meant he ran to the inside door and threw up on the carpet. Our vet determined that Huck had ulcers, which were exacerbated whenever I went out of town, left Huck at home for the day, or even went to the next room without letting him know.

Despite his ulcers, Huck did not have a discriminating palate. He would eat whatever he could find, and it actually didn't even matter if it was meant to be edible. He liked poop—his and others'. Marbles, apples, and avocadoes were big favorites, but tampons, spare change, crayons, anything growing in the vegetable garden, stuffed animals, and whatever else caught his fancy also appealed. Huck never bothered with chewing for the sake of destruction—he just ate things, virtually whole. On more then one occasion I stood over a pile of Huck pooh wondering if I could put a beloved and partially digested stuffed animal through the wash. I never did! We used a busy small-town veterinarian who also performed surgeries. So when I would call to see if Huck was going to be okay because, for example, he had just eaten four avocadoes—pits, skin and all—I would usually be patched through to the speakerphone in the surgery. There would be guffaws all around at Huck's latest antics, and I would be reassured once again with a wink and a snigger that "This too would pass."

After one such phone call, Huck came bounding over in his unique running style, which was completely guided by his over-active tail, put his big squishy head in my lap, proceeded to cover me in muddy drool, looked up at me, and smiled (seriously). At that moment, I realized you couldn't help but laugh with Huck, and that was his gift. Getting mad at him didn't do a thing, except make him look at you with his head turned sideways and a quiz-zical look on his face. But laughing with him made him wiggle all the more, which in turn made me laugh all the harder. And laughing at his transgressions was certainly better than crying about them.

Once I was able to see Huck for the gifts he offered instead of the destruction he left in his path, there were even more positives. Gross but true, I don't think I had to vacuum my car the entire time we had Huck. He would eat up every little scrap and crumb dropped by my children, and he would even lick the seats clean as a bonus. Sweeping under high chairs was completely unneces-sary, as was the prewash cycle on the dishwasher. All you had to do was leave the loaded dishwasher open, and Huck would take care of any stuck-on bits. Huck also had a fierce bark, which came from him being scared, not tough. But no one else had to know that, although it was a bit of a giveaway to the neighbors when Huck was barking and cowering at the sight of the sunflowers in our garden.

Huckleberry came to us after the death of our fifteen-year-old Labrador retriever, when we had recently moved far away from family and friends, and I was dealing with depression. I thought we needed a serious, strong, and athletic running dog. But all we truly needed was Huck, who made us see that a smile, a laugh, and unconditional love make just about anything better. All you had to do was smile at Huck, and his tail would thump on the floor. Toss a pizza crust his way or leave a coffee cake within his reach on the table, and he was even happier. But a smile would certainly do.

As it turns out, our high-maintenance dog was able to accomplish great things after all.

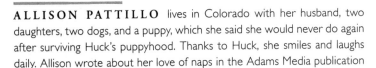

ALLISON PATTILLO lives in Colorado with her husband, two daughters, two dogs, and a puppy, which she said she would never do again after surviving Huck's puppyhood. Thanks to Huck, she smiles and laughs daily. Allison wrote about her love of naps in the Adams Media publication *The Kid Turned Out Fine*.

More Intimidating Than a Plastic Sled

PETE REDINGTON

Kodiak whined excitedly as we fishtailed into the parking lot. The snow was falling heavier than before. As she anxiously offered her best "malamute howl," we trudged through the perfectly light Rocky Mountain powder, arriving at the snowmobile that would (we hoped) carry us the remainder of the journey home: two miles up a snowed-in road that wouldn't be passable again until the mountain flowers were in bloom, sometime in July.

Fortunately, the snowmobile started right up. Unfortunately, the trail had become nearly impossible to see. Sighing with uncertainty, I was distracted by Kodiak, who happily stuck her head in the snow, smelling for, looking at . . . who knows.

I called for her and gunned the heavy Polaris sled forward. She sprinted behind me as usual.

Fifty feet later I stopped, grabbed my goggles out of my backpack, placed them in the more useful location over my previously blinded eyes, and gunned the sled forward again.

Fifty feet later, I stopped again. The snowmobile, having no regular headlight setting, was always set on high beams. The combination of bright lights and the now-heavy snow made the trail virtually impossible to distinguish from the ravine that led so suddenly, and so definitively, down to the frozen stream below.

Still warm from the heat of the car, the pulls of the snowmobile cord, and the eagerness to get home, I wondered what to do. I tried to imagine the trail in my mind's eye. How many turns were there? How many steep climbs up a hill? Kodiak caught up to the stationary snowmobile, leaning in to sniff my leg, making sure everything was all right. Was everything all right? A cold wind slapped my face. Time to get going.

Still searching for answers, I stared dejectedly at my seemingly more menacing surroundings.

Kodiak was a little ahead of the snowmobile now, still sniffing about, looking every bit the sled dog that made her ancestors famous. And I began to wonder whether she might do more than just look the part.

I had never taught her a command to lead. Or even the famous "go home." Who teaches their dog to "go home"? And what dog would actually "go home" and leave her people? Kodiak would just look up at me, confused. *What do you mean go home?* she would wonder. *My home is wherever you are. I am home.*

About a month earlier, I had tied her to a plastic sled to see her demonstrate that instinctive pulling trait that I had read about in various dog books. After a few minutes spent desperately trying to get away from the intimidating piece of plastic that continued to follow her wherever she went, she gave up and lay down.

But lost in the snow, what else could I try?

"Go on!" I yelled to her.

She looked back, confused.

"Go on!" I yelled again, this time motioning my hand outward, toward the trail, like I was shooing away starving mosquitoes.

I accelerated the snowmobile at her. She jumped forward a bit.

"Go on!" I stuck with my mosquito-shooing motion.

Kodiak jumped forward more. I accelerated more. She trotted a bit, looking back at me for approval, or at least to make sure I was going with her. I accelerated a bit more. Her trot turned into a gallop. I followed on the snowmobile. Slowly. Steadily.

Though I couldn't see her furry white tail too well, I could make out her paw prints in the powder that separated us, and they, alone, become my road map. As long as I concentrated on her trail, the blinding snow diving into the high beams didn't seem as blinding.

Imagining a snowmobile to be a bit more intimidating than a plastic sled, I was careful not to get too close. Kodiak was careful to continue to look back, making sure I was following, making sure she was going the right way. *Was* she going the right way? At this point, I had no idea where Kodiak was leading us. I only knew that as long as I could manage to follow her, we could cling to hope.

The dog seemed to understand what she was doing, though. A little.

We climbed up a steep incline, winds blowing in every direction. It was disorienting, as if we were driving in circles—the trail hidden somewhere under the snowdrifts. But Kodiak's paw prints continued, and like a sailor lost in a storm on a foggy night, I continued to head in the same direction as her paw prints—and the promise of safety. A slight turn to the right. A heavy bank to the left. I squinted to see Kodiak's marks in the snow. Onward and upward we went. Slowly. Cautiously. Hopefully.

It seemed to be working. Was it really working?

With each stride, Kodiak was running faster and faster. I imagined her crossing the Yukon River, darting over the tundra, howling toward the finishing line of The Iditarod. Nose to the wind. Heart pumping. Muscles flexing.

Suddenly, she darted left, onto what appeared to be a street now covered in snowdrifts. I careened the snowmobile behind her and cranked the accelerator. The heavy machine managed to spring up, back on the trail. We rounded the final bend, and at last the cabin came into view, appearing like a mirage through the storm.

I passed the shack, headed out onto the frozen pond, turned the snowmobile around (always facing downhill, especially with tonight's storm), cut the engine, and just sat there. Smiling. Stunned. We made it home.

Kodiak wandered over to find me sitting there still. She sniffed at me, wagging her tail. I wondered if she knew what she had just accomplished, or if she was merely happy to sprint through the snow.

PETE REDINGTON no longer inhabits a shack in the mountains of Colorado. He lives in the woods of western Massachusetts with his wife, baby son, and dog Kodiak. His work has appeared in the *Valley Advocate* and *In These Times*.

Love, Seven-Fold

LAD MOORE

I heard a thump and a whimper followed by a screech of automobile tires. I stood up from my deck chair, knowing what the sound meant. As if bathed in hot wax, my face and neck burned with fear as I ran toward the street. At the foot of my driveway, a sobbing woman bent over the hood of her car. At the curb lay "Nacho," the little tan terrier we had rescued from the grips of the pound only three weeks before.

The woman apologized in broken sentences, explaining how the dog ran in front of the car, having been obscured by the two trash bins. But it was my fault. I didn't see Nacho following me when I placed the bins at the curb.

I found myself hugging this total stranger, hushing her halting words that were drowning in tears. She handed me a beach towel, and I wrapped Nacho in its Downy fragrance. I made a coffin from planks left over from a fence I had finished the day before—a fence ironically intended to keep Nacho safe. I set about carving his name and age on the coffin. Pausing at his age for a moment, I wondered if I should adjust it by those "dog years" we all hear and sometimes joke about. I decided no, because to me he was just a pup.

Two years passed before the family could again consider a pet. But a visit to the pound was all it took to reawaken the special bond that only a dog owner knows. The cages were alive with yelping puppies and mature dogs touting their wares. It was as if each was a huckster in a bazaar, competing for a single customer.

We roamed around the kennels as though loose in a candy store, each of our family members reporting what they saw.

"This one has one blue eye and one brown eye," my twelve-year-old shouted.

"Hey! There's a momma dog here with three pups. Can we have all of them?" Then my youngest son explained his reasoning—a family shouldn't be broken apart.

My wife, Kay, announced a candidate: "This is a Dalmatian, I think. He has spots just like the firetruck dogs have." I walked over and looked down at his feet as he waved his tail like the perfect beat of a metronome.

"Look at the size of those paws! They look like baseball mitts! He's going to be way bigger than a Dalmatian, honey. We better keep looking."

Then the magic happened. All four of us were separately drawn to the cage containing a black and white spotted, long-haired puppy. The sign on the cage, written in black marker, read: "Mother was a Lhasa Apso, Father was a traveling man." We had to part his hair even to see his tiny, beady eyes. Our collective gazes met, and the decision was made.

There's something special about adoption from the pound. Maybe it's the heartstrings being stretched to the limit, knowing the ultimate fate of unclaimed dogs and cats. Perhaps it's the satisfaction of granting the second chance that every living thing deserves. On the ride home, we all took turns suggesting names for the newest member of our family.

"I want to call him Puppy Moore," said my youngest.

"I like the name Cosmo," my wife offered. "like the glossy fashion magazine."

"No, let's call him Topper," my oldest son wailed, "Like the bearded man on TV that plays a ghost. He looks like a ghost with his face masked with hair."

We batted those names and others around for thirty minutes. Finally, the role of "Father" had to be invoked. My wife suggested I make the decision, since I hadn't offered up a name.

"Okay then, his name is Cosmo Topper Puppy Moore." Who says that democracy can't be all things to all people?

Eventually his everyday name evolved to Cosmo for brevity. But we still used his complete name when introducing him to friends, because it sounded so aristocratic.

The boys and I took over the training. First the crate, so he would learn that his business was to be done outside. Then followed the tricks all dogs must endure, answering to the commands: "Sit," "Lay," "Heel," "Shake," and "Speak." Cosmo very quickly mastered these tasks. He was so bright I could almost sense him yawning at the lack of challenge.

Twice a week I washed the deck off with the water hose and spray nozzle. As I whipped the hose back and forth to gain slack, I noticed Cosmo following its movements frantically. I joined in the fun, saying, "Kill the snake!" Cosmo would attack the hose, clamping it in his mouth and shaking it furiously. Soon I was able to use that command even when the hose was not being used. It proved a great crowd pleaser at cookouts.

"Kill the snake!" I would yell, and Cosmo would leap from the deck and grab the water hose, shaking and dragging it across the lawn. Then I could say "Dead!" and he would lie beside the mortally wounded water hose, daring it to move.

Then I noticed Cosmo was fascinated with the little wheels on the grill. When I moved the grill out from under the eaves to the front of the deck, he would grab at the wheels, and we would engage in a tug-of-war. During these antics I tacked on the phrase, "Move the pit."

Soon, my friends were treated to this new trick. From my place at the patio table, I would calmly say, "Cosmo, move the pit." He would quickly rise, go to the grill, clamp down on a wheel, and drag the grill out from under the eaves, placing it exactly where I wanted it for cooking.

A chorus of "No way!" echoed out into the neighborhood. My friends were so taken with these moves that after periods of separation, when they called the first question would be, "How is the dog that moves the pit?"

All the way back to the time of Nacho, I denied the idea of those so-called "dog years." But dog years are indeed real—they are multiples of ours. I hear people say, "You know that dogs out-age their masters seven years to one." Master is an equally troublesome word to me, because I am Cosmo's partner, not his better. In the vein of dog math, Cosmo has been returning his love seven-fold to that which we gave him. That is the hero I identify in him. A hero displays hard-to-define character, such as the unwavering devotion that dogs give so tirelessly—devotion we don't even have to earn. Even in cases of animal abuse, the tail will wag to welcome a cruel owner home. Even in the most horrid life conditions, they settle for simple bed and breakfast, hoping in their hearts that love will someday follow.

There's a rule that Cosmo Topper Puppy Moore has imbedded in me: Real heroes never ask but always give.

LAD MOORE is a five-time contributor to Adams Media anthologies and has published three short-story collections of his own. His work has been nominated for Best Fiction at the Texas Institute of Letters and has been published in *Chicken Soup for the Soul*, *Virginia Adversaria*, *Pittsburgh Quarterly*, and numerous other print and online venues. He resides in the historic town of Jefferson, Texas.

Life, A.D. (After Dog)

JAY MAX KRAIDMAN

Some reincarnation theorists claim that in heaven, before we are born, we choose the families and the lives we want to lead before sliding back down the proverbial rainbow chute. If that is the case, then there are truly no accidents. (Though I am sure there are many who are shouting: What were we thinking!)

While that might be a handy ideology to keep in your pocket for a rainy day, when that rainy day turns into a hurricane of illness and financial ruin, even the light of that wishful star can quickly fade.

Such was my family's life for more than ten years. They were years rich in love, though devoid of much else. A chronic disorder had made life physically torturous for my father and emotionally so for my mother. My younger sister and I were thrown into the disorienting position of being in two places at the same time: childhood and adulthood. Over time, we became accustomed to the sad order of things that, preordained or not, felt inescapable.

Then one day, without any conscious plan, a trip to the North Shore Animal League changed everything. We noticed an eight-week-old boxer puppy, the color of liquid caramel, sleeping on someone else's shoulder. We figured that person was going to adopt him. How could anyone resist? My father asked if he could hold him, and amazingly the person said yes.

At that moment, the large room in which we stood disappeared. It seemed to us instead that we were floating on a river, which was gently leading us away from everything we knew for sure—save one thing: the newest member of our family was with us, and we would *never* let him go.

This derailment, so to speak, is where the real story begins. Although our lives remained quantifiably similar, we began to experience little miracles. In Judaism, the story of Chanukah revolves, in essence, around a candle that stayed lit longer than possible.

Something like that has happened to us during these Skippy-filled years. My father, who has always been severely allergic to dogs, has experienced not even a sniffle. (We knock on wood, of course.) A rush of maternal instinct has led my mother back from the dark, into a land of squeaky toys and poop bags. And my sister and I have found a new center, a reason to call our house home and mean it.

Laughter fills each room where Skippy lies on his back, trying to grab his tail. (His uncut tail and ears, we feel sure, are a kind of perfection not meant for human tampering.) We realize, as most true dog lovers do, that Skippy owns us, more than we own him—and that maybe he even chose us.

In return for the unlimited bounty of our love, Skippy, our family's miracle, has kept the light in our life burning longer than we had ever thought possible, B.D: Before Dog.

Now, A.D., things just keep getting better. Skippy's coat is the same sweet shade, and when his regal gold eyes look at you, you hope the person he sees is who you really are. Although we've had to move several times before settling where we are, our one constant has been Skippy. Along the way, he's charmed people out of lifelong dog phobias, given the lonely elderly their first real smile in weeks, and earned us a certain popularity. We've had to get used to being the relatives of a celebrity: people wave mostly to him and greet me unapologetically, "You're Skippy's brother, right?"

Having Skippy in my life has profoundly changed my sense of self. You never quite know how much you can take, until you are pushed to your limits, or how much you can give. I have made the dazzling discovery that there's no limit on our capacity to unselfishly love another being.

There was a time when even a raging fire might not have been enough to get me out of bed in the middle of the night, but for Skippy, a late-night walk is no problem. I play when I'm sad, walk when I'm exhausted, and succumb to joy when every voice in my head tells me I shouldn't. Except for one voice—and it's more of a bark, really.

Sometimes I feel that Skippy would have been fundamentally the same no matter which family had adopted him. Maybe that's not true. I hope that our love—talking to him as if he understood every word and showing him the kindness that we have—has helped create the gentle soul that takes up all of the bed. Either way, one thing is certain: with Skippy in our lives, we have changed for the better and continue to do so every day.

If you stop and think about it, it's freaky. In a world rife with misunderstanding between members of the same species, I know the difference between Skippy's whine for a cheese bone or the one that means I should get into bed so he can cuddle with me. Then again, maybe it's not so strange. Perhaps dogs and people share a universal language that is clearer than any words.

And in that language, ten years, eight weeks, and one day ago, I believe that a pure light chose us to be his family. So with the only language I know, in the only way I know how, I just want to say, thank you.

JAY MAX KRAIDMAN is a writer/artist living on Long Island whose work appears on greeting cards and giftware items, and who is excited to have ventured into the field of product design. Skippy is a superstar/model whose work appears wherever he feels like it, and who splits his time juggling multiple girlfriends, hanging with his friends and in exchange for helping Jay come up with ideas, forces him to carry an embarrassingly large stuffed animal on all their walks. Both can be reached at *JayMax@hotmail.com*.

Dogs Know Things

THOMAS SMITH

Dogs know things. I don't mean things like current political theory, the internal workings of a fuel-injection system, or the answer to most calculus problems (though I have seen a dog who could bark the correct answer if asked the sum of *two plus two*, *three plus one*, or the answer to *one hundred divided by twenty-five* . . . okay, he always barked four times in a row, but it's a neat trick).

No, dogs know important things. They know about unconditional love. Loyalty. Devoted companionship. And they know something about healing the human heart.

My wife and I have two springer spaniels. Arde (pronounced AR-Dee) is the older of the two, liver and white, and a canine clown if ever there was one. Her sister, Corey, is black and white, a year younger, and the more solitary of the two. For the first three years, neither was what you would call a lap dog. Arde would sit very close to my wife, and Corey would lie at my feet, especially when I was at my desk, writing. But they never cared to be on anyone's lap. Arde would tolerate it for a few minutes and then hop down and resume her close-sitting posture.

Corey would just squirm and bolt. All that changed overnight.

My wife and I had moved from South Carolina back to our native North Carolina when her father became ill. My wife is a nurse practitioner, and when we learned her father, Richard, had developed a brain tumor, we sold the house, called the movers, and headed back home.

My father-in-law had always been active in work and play. He could fix anything with a motor, keep a Volkswagen running with a paper clip and two rubber bands, and had been a fireman most of his life. He was a waterman and loved to go out in the boat and work his fishing nets. By the time the tumor was diagnosed, he had begun to tire easily and had to take constant breaks to complete tasks he used to complete with ease. He had also learned the therapeutic benefit of a recliner.

He was reclining when we arrived at their home with our two dogs. Arde and Corey stood and looked at Richard for a moment. Then, without a word (or a woof), Arde very calmly climbed onto Richard's lap and promptly went to sleep.

My in-laws had been around the dogs before, and they were accustomed to the sitting-close-and-stretching-out-at-your-feet routine. But none of us was ready for this.

You see, dogs know things. They know when we are happy. They know when we are sad. They know when we need to scratch them behind the ears and see that goofy dog grin. And they know when there is something *not quite right* with us. Dogs are nature's physicians of the heart, and their medicine is powerful indeed.

Over the next day or so, my father-in-law learned about something else. He learned that a dog in your lap—even a sixty-pound "born-again lap dog"—is good medicine. Arde would gently climb on Richard's lap once he settled in the recliner to rest and watch John Wayne (Richard also learned the therapeutic value of the Western channel on TV), and he would stay until Richard needed to get up. Sometimes they sat there for hours at a time, with Arde receiving almost constant rubbing and Richard receiving something no one else could give.

Then Corey decided to get in on the act. One afternoon, Corey walked over to the front door and started to bark. Not the bark that meant *I'm bored and need something to do.* This was the full-fledged *Danger . . . Danger Will Robinson* bark. Arde woke up, looked around, leaped off Richard's lap, joined Corey, and started barking at the door too. Then, before anyone could get to the door to see what caused the barking, Corey walked over, climbed onto Richard's lap, licked his hand, and went to sleep.

We were stunned (including Arde, I think). Then the four of us laughed like we hadn't laughed in years. But that was just the beginning.

After a couple of days of the barking-at-the-door ruse, followed by Corey's stealthy climb onto Richard's lap, the tables turned. One Saturday afternoon, Arde stood up, ran to the door, and started barking as if Nazi storm troopers were charging the front porch. Corey jumped down, ran to the door, and joined in at the top of her lungs. At which time Arde trotted over, climbed in her accustomed spot, and went to sleep.

About eighteen months later, my wife's father died. He was at home where he wanted to be, but he was so frail that the dogs couldn't get on the bed with him. Still, they maintained their vigil, settling for waiting in the hall. Sometimes they slept just outside the door, occasionally going in, making a circuit of the room, and then going back into the hall.

On the day Richard died, Arde and Corey stood in the hall-way watching the coming and going of hospice workers, EMTs, family, and friends. They didn't bark. They didn't beg for treats. They just watched. Then, after the funeral, after everyone had gone and we were alone, Arde walked into the room . . . and immediately climbed onto my mother-in-law's lap.

You see, dogs know things.

THOMAS SMITH is an award-winning writer, reporter, TV news producer, essayist, and playwright. Most important, he has been the play-mate of several good dogs over the years, including the two in this story. He is married to the woman who hung the moon and is also a pretty fair banjo picker.

Sunday Mornings with Duke

STEPHEN BLACKBURN

Duke was a mongrel, most likely the product of an illicit affair between a sweet young Collie and a boofhead Labrador. He had a short, stubby, black and white body supported by short, stubby, black and white legs.

I was five years old in 1968, the year Duke came to live with my family. The image that still flickers, all these years later, is of this little runt of a pup nuzzling against my knee as I sat cross-legged on the grass, an action he would repeat thousands of times in the next eleven years.

Sundays belonged to Duke and me—Sunday mornings to be exact. No matter the weather, from the age of eight onward, I would leap out of bed just after sunup, dress quickly, and head for the back door. Breakfast could wait. As soon as Duke heard the back door scrape open, he barged from his sleeping box, banging through the outside laundry door and down onto the back veranda, where he sat, his thick tail thumping on the concrete, waiting. I would dutifully scratch him under his chin, pat my hand against my leg, and say, "Come on, Duke, we gotta get my bike." Duke responded with a paroxysm of joy that sent him tearing to the shed, where he knew my pushbike sat among the detritus of my family's life: the cribs, tricycles, and baby clothes packed away in old dusty suitcases, which no longer had a place in the house but could not be discarded. The three of us—a boy, his metal, rubber-wheeled mount, and his dog—headed out, down the side of the house, along the drive and out to the street.

Derry Avenue was a bicyclist's dream. Two miles long, with only a scattering of houses in grouped bunches, it rose, dipped, twisted, and turned. Our house sat a third of the way up a steep hill. As I began our Sunday ritual, pushing the bike up the hill, Duke trotted happily along. At times he bounded ahead to sniff at lampposts or trees, where he relieved himself, marking the territory as his once more, before returning, tail flicking excitedly, to my side. When the road flattened out at the crown, I mounted my blue and white Malvern Star and began pedaling slowly, weaving from side to side. Duke manned his station alongside the pedals, keeping pace, mimicking the same movements the bike and I did. He no longer noticed lampposts and kept his gaze fixed straight ahead. We wheeled along at a lazy, weaving pace until we reached the end of the road. Pausing at Walter Street, I gave Duke a final scratch on his head, our good luck ritual, and then we would take off, me standing, working the pedals hard to pick up speed, and Duke trotting dutifully alongside. We aimed for maximum speed until we reached the downward drop of the hill, so we could flash past our house, down into the dip, where the creek ran under the road, and up the reverse slope without having to touch the pedals again.

During these dashes up and down the twists and turns of Derry Avenue, Duke and I became of one mind. It was all about speed. I hunkered down over the handlebars to streamline myself, against the wind, and Duke became the master of aerodynamics. In spite of his slovenly chunkiness, on Sunday mornings Duke became as sleek as a torpedo. He laid his pointy ears back along his head, thrust his nose forward like the tip of a spear and, with a metamorphic ability, extended that thick body into a tight cylinder. The trot became a hard, full-blown gallop as he propelled himself forward in a valiant attempt to keep pace. His hard breathing melded with the sounds of my own and the hum of the bike's tires as they sped madly over the asphalt. It was nothing short of grand—a boy and his dog, as one.

These pursuits of speed continued for an hour or two until I finally gave in and slashed the bike in a wide curve back into our driveway. The bike and I collapsed onto the lawn, where I heaved to catch my breath. Duke, after lapping at the bowl under the dripping tap at the back of the outside toilet, nuzzled my knee, and then slumped his fat body down on the grass, resting his head on my leg. As I scratched him behind his ear, he would train his dark, expressive eyes on me, locking them on my face until I broke the spell. Sunday mornings with Duke were simply the best.

Duke would have been eleven or twelve years old when I found him one morning lying in a ditch as I walked to high school. Sometime during the night, on one of his evening lothario visits around the neighborhood, a motorist had apparently struck him. My precious Duke died alone and away from home. As my father buried him in the vacant lot next to our home, I wept unashamedly. I still do.

STEPHEN BLACKBURN lives in Mount Nasura, western Australia, along with his wife, Jennine, and two teenage boys, Aaron and Christian. He is constantly in awe of everyone else's abilities and constantly in despair of his own.

In the Company of Elliott

TRACY GRIMALDI

"**W**ell, what do you think?" I pressed my husband, Paul, for his decision. Our new German shorthaired pointer puppy needed a name. As if he knew I was talking about him, the puppy got up from my lap and rose on his tippy-toes until he looked me square in the face.

"He reminds me of that dragon in the movie *Pete's Dragon*. You know—kind of dumb and goofy-looking," Paul said, laughing.

I gasped and covered the puppy's ears. "He most certainly is not dumb. In just the few days we've had him, I can tell he's very intelligent."

Paul shrugged. "But he does have a goofy way about him. I think that dragon's name was Elliott." Paul cupped the puppy's chin in his hand and gazed into his large brown eyes. "I think Elliott fits him."

"Okay." I picked up the puppy and whispered in his ear, "I love you, Elliott."

He licked my nose and then settled once again on my lap. Soon the room filled with the sound of contented puppy snores.

As Elliott grew, so did his awareness of household employment opportunities. His first self-appointed position was as Kitty Bottom Examiner, much to the cat's dismay. Despite her swat-of-the-paw disapproval, his proboscis tried to explore this aromatic territory with a Lewis and Clark-like passion.

Never fully retiring from that job, Elliott promoted himself to Director of Special Ops, specializing in covert maneuvers. One day he approached me as I sat on the sofa.

"Woof, woof. Woof, woof, woof."

I looked up from my book. "What is it, boy?"

Elliott weaved through the family room as if on an obstacle course. Once clear, he charged to the kitchen, ran back to me, and barked again. His loud and insistent bark conveyed a "you need to come now" urgency.

Thoughts of old Lassie movies flashed through my mind. Lassie, at the risk of her own well-being, always warned of impending danger. What was Elliott trying to communicate?

"What's wrong? Show me." I jumped up and headed toward the kitchen. Elliott pushed past me then came to a full point. I followed his gaze to the countertop. Nestled in a dark corner sat the culprit—an errant biscuit.

Elliott continued on his career quest. Hours spent waiting at the door for me to come home from work added Good Friend to his resume. His desire to be only at my side put Faithful Companion on the list too.

But there was one occupation that seemed to be Elliott's highest calling. True to his namesake, Elliott's finest hours were as a Big Goofball. He seemed to derive his greatest pleasure from causing laughter.

One cold winter morning, I scuffled downstairs in my robe and an oversized pair of wooly socks. Elliott grabbed a chew toy and occupied himself in front of the glowing fireplace while I sipped my coffee. He cast a furtive glance in my direction. "You want to come up here?" I patted the spot next to me.

Elliott looked at me, and then went back to gnawing on his toy.

Soon, he shot me another look, turning away when my eyes caught his. It was as if he were planning something. Suddenly, he bolted, and lightning-quick, snatched the lumpy end of my too-big sock and tugged.

"Hey." I held on to the sock. "Stop it."

With no regard to my command, he pulled harder, wrangling the prized possession off my foot. I lunged toward the sock, managed to grasp it and refused to let go while Elliott dragged me across the floor. "Elliott, no," I gasped through my laughter.

Spurred on by my giggles, he pranced across the room, tossing my sock up into the air like a circus juggler.

It wasn't until my brother, Noel, came to visit that the depth of Elliott's mission in life was revealed. When he arrived, Noel seemed surrounded by a cloud of sadness. Shattered dreams, lost love, and broken promises fractured his heart and eradicated his usual joyfulness. Sojourning and searching brought him to my doorstep.

Elliott wiggled and jiggled with delight when he was introduced to Noel. He covered Noel's face with slobbery kisses. Elliott followed my brother from room to room while I gave a tour of the house, and then he settled on the sofa next to him for the rest of the evening. As the days passed, although Elliott always checked in with me as if to assure me of his love, he relished being my brother's constant companion.

When I washed dinner dishes, Elliott curled up next to my brother on the sofa, his head on Noel's lap. It became a familiar sight, except now the once-hard lines that defined my brother's face softened. Mornings, Noel descended the stairs whistling from a song that filled his heart.

One day after Noel settled down to read the newspaper, Elliott occupied a spot on the floor an unusual distance away. Odd, I thought, until I noticed my brother wiggling his toes inside a large pair of socks. Elliott observed the movement with a nonchalant manner as if it were just one of many things going on around him.

I knew better.

"You better watch out. Elliott likes to . . ." Before I could finish, Elliott charged, snatched, and tugged the sock on my brother's foot.

What happened next was like watching something from an old cartoon. They tussled, rumbled, rolled, and spun. When the dust settled, Elliott emerged with the sock in his mouth and Noel with a tear-stained face, gasping with laughter.

When my brother left to go home, he was a changed man, transformed by a magical dog named Elliott.

Upon first meeting, Elliott appeared to be a silly, lovable, self-promoting dog full of goofball antics, but his supreme calling ran much deeper. Elliott was a Protector of the Heart and Guardian of the Soul. His life seemed complete only when those around him were complete. One could never be the same after spending time in the company of Elliott.

TRACY GRIMALDI'S writing credits include online publications in *Pen Pricks*, *Moondance Magazine* and *A Long Story Short*. Her awards include winnings in the True Life Story Contest and the Christopher Newport University Writers' Conferences. She considers one of her highest honors the unconditional love and faithfulness lavished on her by a goofy dog named Elliott.

Bumbo the Wonder Dog

KATHRYN THOMPSON PRESLEY

Old Jumbo was a handsome boxer, gifted at herding cows and generally helping my father around the farm. Large and muscled, with the intelligence common to his breed, our boxer soon became a valued member of the family. In their lonely little "shotgun" cabin high above the Washita River, my parents had only each other and old Jumbo for company. They had long since given up on having children, so it was a shock to all three when I made my appearance in the worst year of the Depression, amid Oklahoma's Dust Bowl.

At first, Jumbo refused to acknowledge me. He would get up and slink away if they brought me out on the porch, and he refused to come into the house until winter's icy grip finally drove him to the fire. One of my first memories was the sound of Jumbo's gentle snoring as he slept on the rug beside my crib. Papa had "jerry rigged" the crib from orange crates. My first word was "Bumbo" as I tried unsuccessfully to wrap my toddler tongue around the dog's name. "Bumbo" he remained for the rest of his life. By then, he had become my protector and best friend. Years later, when reading *Peter Pan*, I had no difficulty believing in Nana, the canine nursemaid, for Bumbo had been my guardian for the first six years of my life.

While they did the milking, my parents placed me in an orange crate just outside the feedlot, with Bumbo guarding me. He faithfully let them know when danger approached–once he snapped the head off an approaching chicken snake; mostly he drove off aggressive geese. And when I began to walk, he would grasp my shirt in his mouth and bark vigorously if I wandered too far from the house. With the Washita River on one side, the Santa Fe Railroad track on the other, and a busy highway not far away, it was not a safe environment for toddlers. My parents learned to trust Bumbo implicitly.

I don't remember my first and only swim in the Washita River. My parents said it was the hottest summer in memory and they decided to take a swim in the twilight. I was only six months old, so they parked me on a pallet on the riverbank, leaving Bumbo to guard me, as usual. They heard the first splash when I decided to join them and sank like lead in the muddy water. The second splash was Bumbo to the rescue. He came up holding the straps of my sunsuit tightly in his teeth while I squalled loudly. It was my parents' last swim in the river. (Papa always teased I got my red hair from that swim in the murky red waters of the Washita.)

I do remember, vividly, the angry bull who charged me as I toddled around the place. Old Bumbo tore into him like a swarm of angry hornets, diverting him until my father arrived to take charge.

Cotton was our main cash crop, so my parents worked long hours in the cotton fields, though the return was meager in those Dust Bowl years. During my first and second cotton-picking season, my parents parked me under a cottonwood tree in a make-shift playpen lined with quilts, assigning Bumbo to watch over me. His job grew more difficult as I began to toddle around the farm, tormenting old setting hens, chasing turkeys, and being chased by belligerent geese.

Bumbo remained my nursemaid and friend until he died just before my sixth birthday. My parents were bereft and dreaded telling me. It must have broken their hearts to hear me calling his name piteously as I searched every place I could think of where he might be hiding. Finally, Papa saddled his old plow horse and, with me clasping his waist, rode out into the pasture to a mound of red Oklahoma clay which was obviously, even to my young eyes, a grave.

"Papa, do you think that's old Bumbo?" I asked, quavering. He reckoned it might be. When I asked the age-old question, "Do dogs go to heaven?" he did his best to comfort me.

"Honey, if any dog makes it to heaven, you can be sure Bumbo will be the one."

I clung to that in the following months, as we left the farm forever, finally defeated by the mortgage. We moved to the city, where our cramped little apartments were not amenable to pets. It would be years before I had another dog. Meanwhile, I delighted in sitting on the front porch, regaling the neighborhood children with embellished stories of Bumbo—how he had saved me from poisonous snakes, tornadoes, tarantulas, scorpions, stampeding cattle, rabid coyotes . . . and even dragged me from burning buildings.

Astonished, Mama called me inside one day. "Kathryn Jane, Bumbo was a wonderful dog, but aren't you stretching the truth just a little bit? You make him sound like 'Bumbo the Wonder Dog—faster than a speeding bullet, more powerful than a locomotive, able to leap tall buildings in a single bound.'"

"I know, Mama, but I just want them all to know Bumbo was a GREAT dog, the best dog who ever lived."

I suppose many of us have "memory places" to which we escape when life closes in on us—in the dentist's chair, in hospital waiting rooms. For seventy years, my time and place has been cold winter nights in that tiny shotgun cabin on the banks of the Washita. Outside the prairie winds howl around the eaves, eggs freeze and pop under the bed. But I'm snug and secure as the wood stove sends out its warmth, throwing shadows on the ceiling. And I know no harm can ever befall me while Bumbo the Wonder Dog snores softly beside me.

KATHRYN THOMPSON PRESLEY is a freelance writer living in Bryan, Texas. She has two grown children, four grandchildren, and a great-grandson. She enjoys reading, READING, READING, and playing Scrabble with her grandchildren.

A Letter to My Running Partner

CATHARINE MOSER

Dear Ebbe,

Because you ignore the English language no matter how loudly I speak it to you whenever we go for a run, I thought I might communicate more effectively with you if I wrote down my thoughts in a letter.

We've gone running on most mornings for all of your three years. For you to whine, race around the living room (we have looped carpet in there—do you know that your claws pull up those little loops?), and smash your body against me while I try to lace up my running shoes is obnoxious and ridiculous. Besides, I hate picking off, one at a time, those strands of long, white, soft fur you leave on my black leggings.

Have you noticed yet that we run every *other* day? On off days we're allowed to sleep past our normal running time. Kindly stop sticking your nose in my face and snuffling because your internal clock says it's time to get up and run. Can't you ever enjoy a day off?

Here's a news flash: Deer have lived in this valley for eons. They have a right to cross the road ahead of us, or browse in the hayfield next to us, or stare at us and try to figure out what the heck we're doing outside of a car. Your growling and woofing at them interrupts the tranquility of our morning runs through the valley. Besides, as a protector, you're about as dangerous as a robin. I've seen you rush the UPS driver when he pulls into the driveway to deliver a package. You wag your tail, and I know you beg him for a treat and some petting.

And another thing: Will you ever get savvy about cars and pickup trucks? You really should make an effort to come to me at once when I holler, "Ebbe, COME!" instead of standing serenely in the middle of the road watching the rigs approach, slowly wagging your tail! Now have you guessed why I leash you when we run that stretch of road that winds alongside the beaver ponds? It's that series of blind curves that got my imagination going— imagining an English setter flat as a pancake on asphalt. I have to say, though, you've been a good sport about the leashing.

Could you please stay on the road and out of the ditches? That lovely, flowing, silky fur on those floppy ears of yours collects every kind of plant matter known to man. Ditto about the feathering on your tail, legs, and belly. We're *running*, not hunting! In the autumn, when you're working the fields hunting birds, there's not a thing I can do about the cockleburs, twigs, and hound's-tongue seeds hitching a ride on that pretty white, black, and tan coat of yours. That's why on those days I don't grumble so much about having to brush out the mess.

And about the pointing: *Must* you stop to point birds when we run? Yes, you're first a hunting dog, then a running partner. You will always be faithful to scenting and pointing birds. But I'm a runner before I'm a hunter. I like the challenge of trying to shave away seconds from the usual two hours it takes us to run from home to the graveyard and back, but you insist on stopping to point every grouse and pheasant we come upon. And because I'm a conscientious, dutiful owner of an English setter, I do hold up our run and simulate a hunt in the field with you, walking toward the birds until they flush. Well, poof! There goes any chance of paring down our running time.

Actually, the pointing is pretty cool—you look great! So classic and regal, you're a tribute to your breed. I've pretty much resigned myself to the unlikelihood of ever bettering my time as long as I run with you.

You do aggravate me sometimes, and you don't seem too bright—but you do have your positive attributes. You're the one who loves to snowshoe with me through the forest when winter's snow and ice have laid claim to the road. In March, you'll run with me if it's twenty degrees outside and we have to zigzag to hop over patches of ice and snow still covering the road. You get up with me ungodly early to run in the summer and beat the heat.

Isn't the highlight of our two-hour run reaching the old graveyard? The plump meadowlarks sing and the breeze swirls. When it's just us girls sitting next to Hollis Burton's headstone, I guzzle lemonade and toss you a biscuit. We breathe the aroma of sage and prairie grass that covers the low hills that roll across central Montana. You lie at my side, finally relaxed! My hand strokes the black and tan fur on your head. Your hazel eyes gaze toward the horizon, wondering about birds, of course. I'm sure you'll continue to ignore my commands, and I'm sure you'll insist on pointing birds. Still, you're my running partner, and together we've racked up a lot of miles. And for that, I thank you.

Hey, this morning it's cool, misting and the first of September. Wanna go for a run?

When freelancer **CATHARINE MOSER** and Ebbe are not running loose through central Montana's Judith Mountains, she's writing about Western history, lifestyles and the outdoors for *Runner's World*, *Wild Blue Yonder*, *National Wildlife*, *Western Horseman*, *Western Art & Architecture*, *Persimmon Hill*, *Big Sky Journal*, *High Country News*, *Montana Magazine*, *Signature Montana*, *Fur-Fish-Game*, *Antique Trader*, and *Seattle Homes & Lifestyles*.